Joe DiMaggio

Read all of the books in this exciting,
action-packed biography series!

Hank Aaron

Barry Bonds

Joe DiMaggio

Tim Duncan

Dale Earnhardt Jr.

Lou Gehrig

Derek Jeter

Michelle Kwan

Mickey Mantle

Jesse Owens

Ichiro Suzuki

Tiger Woods

SPORTS HEROES AND LEGENDS™

Joe DiMaggio

by Kevin Viola

Lerner Publications Company/Minneapolis

For my mom

Lerner Publications Company
A division of Lerner Publishing Group
241 First Avenue North
Minneapolis, MN 55401 U.S.A.

Website address: www.lernerbooks.com

Cover photograph:
© Bettmann/CORBIS

Library of Congress Cataloging-in-Publication Data

Viola, Kevin, 1974–
    Joe DiMaggio / by Kevin Viola.
        p.   cm. — (Sports heroes and legends)
    Includes bibliographical references and index.
    ISBN-13: 978-0-8225-3081-7 (lib. bdg. : alk. paper)
    ISBN-10: 0-8225-3081-3 (lib. bdg. : alk. paper)
    1. DiMaggio, Joe, 1914–1999—Juvenile literature. 2. Baseball players—United States—Biography—Juvenile literature. I. Title. II. Series.
GV865.D5V56 2006
796.357′092—dc22   2004029287

Manufactured in the United States of America
1 2 3 4 5 6 – JR – 11 10 09 08 07 06

J B
DIMAGGIO J
C. 1

Contents

Prologue
The Unbeatable Streak
1

Chapter One
Young Joe
6

Chapter Two
Jolly Days
13

Chapter Three
A Major League Deal
19

Chapter Four
The Next Babe
28

Chapter Five
A New Star in Town
38

Chapter Six
Joltin' Joe
48

Chapter Seven
In the Army Now
58

Chapter Eight
Back in the Game
65

Chapter Nine
Lucky to Be a Yankee
79

Chapter Ten
Two Great Loves
87

Epilogue
A Hero Lives On
93

Personal Statistics
98

Batting Statistics
99

Fielding Statistics
100

Sources
101

Bibliography
102

Websites
104

Index
105

The Unbeatable Streak

In the summer of 1941, the unthinkable was happening. The New York Yankees were slumping—big time. After winning the World Series four years in a row from 1936 to 1939, the Yanks had come in third in 1940. Everyone had thought it was a fluke. Certainly the team would come back like wildfire in 1941. The fans were counting on it.

By the end of April, the Yankees were in third again. By the end of May, they had slipped to fourth and just kept on losing. No one on the team could hit—not even the team's hero, center fielder Joe DiMaggio. From the last week of April through the first two weeks of May, the mighty Joe DiMaggio had a batting average of .194. He might as well have been a Little League player facing big league pitchers.

When Joe hit a single in a game against the Chicago White Sox on May 15, no one thought it was a big deal. The Yankees went on to lose the game—their fifth-straight loss—by a horrific score of 13–1. The next day, Joe hit a home run against the White Sox. The day after that, it was a single. The following day, Joe had three hits in three at bats against the St. Louis Browns. A hitting streak was beginning, but no one knew it yet. Fans and sportswriters alike were just happy that Joe was doing something good for the team.

Joe's batting average rose steadily out of the gutter, climbing to .330 by Memorial Day. Still, no one really noticed until he started closing in on the Yankee record for longest hitting streak. The record had been set first by Roger Peckinpaugh in 1919 and then tied by Earle Combs in 1931. It stood at twenty-nine games.

In mid-June, the Cleveland Indians came to New York, and each team was building a winning streak. The Yankees had won five straight; the Indians had won six. But in the first game of the three-game series, the Yankees showed the visitors who was boss. Joe hit a run-scoring double in the third inning, and the Yankees won 4–1. Joe's streak was at twenty-seven. The next day, the Yankees beat the Indians again, and this time Joe hit a huge home run.

On Monday, June 16, Joe was set to tie the Yankee hitting streak record. But stormy skies almost ended the whole thing. During the fifth inning, it started raining so hard the game was almost called, and DiMaggio had yet to get his hit. But it stopped raining as quickly as it had started and in his next at bat, Joe slapped out a double. He had tied the Yankee record!

After that, the press was all wrapped up in the streak. Everyone was talking about the remaining hitting records. George Sisler held the Major League Baseball record with a forty-one-game streak in 1922. Longer than that was the all-time streak of forty-four games set in 1887 by Wee Willie Keeler. But this mark had been set before foul balls were even called as strikes. Could Joe break those records? Could this be history in the making?

As Joe kept hitting straight through June, the entire country got caught up in streak fever. In 1941 Major League Baseball had no teams in the western United States. In fact, the St. Louis Browns were the westernmost team in the league. But people from Texas to Montana to Joe's home state of California were reading about the streak in newspapers. Radio stations would interrupt their programs to let fans know that Joe had just made another hit. Joe had been a New York hero since his rookie season in 1936, but the streak was making him a national hero.

Finally the day came for Joe to tie and possibly beat George Sisler's major league record. It was June 29, and the Yankees were in Washington, D.C., for a doubleheader against the Senators. The fans were going crazy, trying to get onto the field for pregame batting practice. Joe had to be escorted to warm-ups by the police. The stadium sold out and the Senators' manager, Bucky Harris, knew there was only one reason. "We couldn't even draw flies for a few games before the Yankees came to town," he said.

In the first game, Joe's first at bat came in the second inning. Joe connected, but he lined out. In the fourth, he hit a pop-up to third and was out again. Then in the sixth, he hit a double to left center and the crowd went nuts. Joe stepped on second base and took a deep breath. He had tied the major league batting record! Next he just had to top it. Since the team still had one more game to play that day, the goal was within reach. But then everything changed.

Between the two games of the doubleheader, Joe's favorite bat was stolen from the dugout. An usher told Joe that some kid had just leaned over, grabbed it, and disappeared into the crowd before anyone could catch him. Joe, like many ballplayers, was very superstitious. What was he going to do without his streak bat? Joe had no choice but to take the field with a replacement bat and hope for the best. But it wasn't enough. Joe was shaken.

Joe stepped up to the plate in the first inning and hit a line drive to right. It was an easy out. In the third inning, he hit a line drive to shortstop for another easy out. In the fifth, he hit a fly ball that was caught with no problem. Could this really be the end? Then, right before the seventh inning, Joe's teammate Tom Henrich pulled him aside. Back in early June, Joe had loaned Tommy one of his bats. Henrich returned it, hoping it might bring the magic back.

Joe took the field with his old bat. The first pitch that came to him was high and inside—ball one. On the second pitch, Joe swung and smacked the ball into left field. Joe dashed to first and the crowd went crazy. He probably could have made it to second base, but his legs were shaking too much.

Joe went on to beat Keeler's all-time record on July 2 with a home run against the Boston Red Sox. All in all, it wasn't bad for a shy, scrawny kid from the streets of San Francisco.

Chapter | One

Young Joe

Joseph Paul DiMaggio was born on November 25, 1914, in Martinez, California. His father, Giuseppe DiMaggio, and his mother, Rosalie Mercurio, had met and married in Sicily, Italy, where they were both born and raised. Giuseppe was a fisherman, and in 1898, when his wife was pregnant with their first child, he heard that there was good fishing to be had off the coast of California. Hoping for a better life for his family, Giuseppe left for the United States, thinking he would stay for at least a year and see how things worked out. Rosalie and the baby would live with family until he returned, and Giuseppe would send money back when he could. The fishing business in northern California turned out to be even better than Giuseppe had hoped. He stayed, and four years later he sent for his wife and their young daughter Nellie to join him in the States. The DiMaggios would make a life for themselves in a new country.

The DiMaggio family moved into a two-bedroom house near the water in Martinez—a town just outside the bustling city of San Francisco. The little village was filled with immigrants from Sicily, just like Giuseppe and Rosalie, but it was much more modern than the old-fashioned town the DiMaggios had come from. It had factories and electric streetlights. But fishing was the main trade in town.

When Joe was little, his parents spoke Italian all the time, but Joe never picked it up. He could understand them but couldn't speak it very well. Communication between the two generations was tough until his parents' English improved.

Every morning the men would go out on their boats to fish the open ocean. Giuseppe bought a fishing boat and named it the *Rosalie D*. In his very own vessel he would search the ocean for shad, sturgeon, and sardines. Giuseppe fished six days a week, rising before dawn and coming home in the late afternoon. He made a decent living—enough to keep his small family comfortable in their new home. But his family wouldn't be small for long.

While Giuseppe was fishing, Rosalie cooked, kept the house, and looked after her growing family. First was Nellie, who was born in Sicily. Then came Mamie, Tom, Marie, Michael, Frances, Vince, Joe, and Dominic—nine children in all. Joe was the last child to be born in the Martinez cabin. When Joe was a toddler, Giuseppe decided to move his family into a larger place in the city. Giuseppe found an apartment on Taylor Street in the North Beach section of San Francisco, a place the family would call home for years.

Giuseppe was never a big talker, and Joe took after him in that respect. He was shy as a boy and would never speak to his elders unless spoken to first, and sometimes not even then. But Joe loved living in the city. It was filled with playgrounds and trolley cars, movie theaters and ballparks. A kid could have fun in the city, and Joe and his friends definitely had fun.

Because Joe was so shy, he almost never spoke in class. He was terrified of getting something wrong and being laughed at, so he and his friends would sit in the back of the classroom at Hancock Elementary and mess around for most of the day. Joe earned mediocre grades, and he didn't much like school. It was on the baseball field that he really shone. The oldest DiMaggio boys, Tom and Mike, were both known at the local playgrounds for being great hitters. Of course their little brothers, Vince, Joe, and Dominic, wanted to be just like them, so they all played as much baseball as possible. It became clear early on that the younger boys, especially Joe and Vince, could whack a ball just as far as Mike and Tom could. When Joe's friends picked teams at the park, whoever was lucky enough to get Joe was sure to win. Joe loved hitting the ball over the fence, running the bases, and hearing his friends cheer for him. It was one of the only times he felt really comfortable.

Joe and his friends didn't play baseball all of the time, of course. When they weren't in school or at the North Beach Playground, they rode the cable cars around San Francisco, played cards, and snuck into movies because they didn't have the money to pay for tickets.

In fact, the DiMaggio family didn't have a lot of money to spend on anything. With all those kids to take care of, money was tight. Joe was constantly dressed in hand-me-down clothes and shoes that had been worn so many times by his brothers, his mother had to place cardboard inside to reinforce the soles. As soon as the boys were old enough to work, Giuseppe expected them to join him on the fishing boat.

❝My mother knew how to get the most from a chicken. Nothing went to waste.**❞**
—JOE, TALKING ABOUT THE USE OF LEFTOVERS IN HIS HOUSE

Giuseppe wasn't an overly ambitious man. He didn't expect his kids to go to college and become doctors or teachers or lawyers. In Giuseppe's mind, all that mattered was a hard day's work and putting food on the table for the family. So while Joe was still in school, first Tom and then Mike joined the family business, going to work right after they finished the eighth grade. Joe, however, wasn't looking forward to this fate. Boats made him seasick, and he couldn't stand the smell of fish. The last thing he wanted was to become a fisherman. The problem was, he had no idea *what* he wanted to do.

Joe made it through grade school, but when he reached Galileo High School, it became clear just how little he had learned in his early years. All that goofing around had its price. He couldn't keep up with the advanced classes and even worse, he was required to speak in class. One day, when Joe was fifteen, his Italian teacher teased him for not knowing his verbs. Joe was mortified and angry and, as he always did when he was embarrassed, he blushed furiously, which just humiliated him more. Then the teacher threw him out of class for not doing his homework. Joe was so upset, he never went back. For months he played hooky from school, hanging out with his friends on the streets. (A lot of Joe's friends had either dropped out or played hooky as well.) Finally the school sent a letter home and Joe was caught.

Joe might not have received great grades, but he did win an award for penmanship in grade school.

Joe's older brother Tom was furious at Joe for throwing away his opportunities. He set up a meeting with the school principal and brought Joe along to talk things out. They sat in the waiting area and waited. And waited. The principal never showed up. Finally Joe looked up at his brother and said, "Tom, they don't want me." Tom had to agree it looked that way. He was angry again, but this time at the school. No one treated him and his brother this way. He made Joe promise to take his equivalency exam and get his diploma, but Joe never did. Joe was done with tests, homework, and school.

Giuseppe, of course, expected Joe to get right on the fishing boat and start helping out, but Joe was as reluctant as ever to spend his days on the ocean. Meanwhile Joe's older brother Vince became the first DiMaggio kid to truly rebel. He didn't want to be a fisherman either. He wanted to be a ballplayer. When Giuseppe heard this news, he lost it. Who made money playing games? Nobody Giuseppe knew. Vince had to join the family business and that was that. Against his father's wishes, Vince left home and joined the Lumber Leagues of northern

California, which were the equivalent of the minor leagues in that region. From that moment on, Giuseppe refused to speak to Vince. His son had broken his heart.

Still, even with all the drama and heartache over Vince's decision, it got Joe thinking. If Vince could play baseball for a living, why couldn't Joe do it too?

Chapter | Two

Jolly Days

After Vince left home, Giuseppe tried to force Joe to come out fishing with him, Tom, and Mike. He wasn't going to have another rebel in the family. But Joe resisted, and this time Rosalie stepped in. She couldn't stand the idea of losing another one of her boys. She told Giuseppe to leave Joe alone, that she knew he would become something in time. Joe's mother had faith in him, and that meant a lot to Joe. The only problem was, he had no idea what he wanted to become. Sure, playing baseball for a living was a great idea, but not everyone made it, and Joe hadn't played in a while—he'd been too busy loafing around. Plus Joe looked up to Vince. His big brother was the greatest player he knew—much better than Joe, in Joe's opinion. He wasn't sure he would be good enough to play professional ball.

Unsure of what to do with himself, Joe tried out a few things. He and his little brother, Dominic, had been selling papers on street corners for a while, so he continued to do that. He also tried stacking boxes at a couple of different warehouses, but the work was tough and very boring. He didn't last long at those jobs.

Joe, who was always competitive with his little brother, Dominic, said Dom sold more papers than Joe because he was short and had glasses so people felt sorry for him.

Then in 1931, when Joe was sixteen, one of his old friends, Frank Venezia, asked him if he wanted to join his baseball team, the Jolly Knights. The Knights were a club team that played organized games against other small club and company teams in the San Francisco area. Frank said the Jolly Knights were going to have real uniforms with brand-new shoes and everything. It sounded like a good deal to Joe. After all, Vince had played on a company team for a while, and that was where he had been discovered by a semipro scout. This could be Joe's big shot. At the very least, Joe was going to be playing ball again.

The Jolly Knights played on Saturdays and Sundays, with Joe DiMaggio playing either shortstop or third base. Joe was fast in the field, and every ball he hit was a shot. With his help, the

Knights started winning all over the place, beating almost every team they faced. Their success caught the attention of local companies, and it earned them an official sponsor, the Rossi Olive Oil Company. Getting a sponsor was a big deal. It meant new uniforms and new equipment. The Jolly Knights were on top of the world.

The club team games and their results were often written up in the local papers, and the Knights took up a lot of space on the sports page with their winning ways. Even Vince heard about their success and challenged his little brother's team to a game. The Jolly Knights accepted and went off to play Vince's semipro team, knowing that Vince and his teammates were much better than they. What did the Knights do? They won! They were good enough to beat real, *paid* players. It made Joe wonder why he wasn't being paid to play.

 When Joe was asked to play for the Jolly Knights, he signed on mostly for the free shoes.

In the spring of 1932, the Jolly Knights played a game right before the game of a team sponsored by Sunset Produce. The company's owner saw Joe hitting every pitch that came to him and thought he'd like to have a player like that on his company's team. He offered Joe a few dollars to play in a game with his crew, and Joe was ecstatic. Money for baseball! What could be better?

After that, Joe found himself playing for half a dozen different clubs, all of which were willing to pay him to hit. He worked all summer, playing night games and weekend games, moving from team to team. In the eighteen games he played for Sunset Produce, Joe had an incredible .632 batting average. The Sunset Produce people were so happy, they gave Joe his first pair of real baseball spikes. (Spikes were an early version of baseball cleats.) He was also being written up in the papers more and more as local reporters started to take note of his unbelievable hitting. Maybe Vince wasn't the only DiMaggio with major baseball talent.

Unfortunately, Joe wasn't as great in the field as he was behind the plate. His errors and missed plays frustrated him, so he committed himself to working on his game. He watched other shortstops and studied their moves. He learned to anticipate where the ball would be hit, based on the pitch and the batter's stance. Joe practiced as hard as he could, hoping to become the best player possible. He would accept nothing less. Thanks to this dedication, he steadily improved and became a double threat—great in the field, killer at the plate.

The more attention Joe got from the press, the more he started to think that he might be able to follow in his brother's footsteps, making his living playing baseball. Of course he still had to overcome one major obstacle. Giuseppe hadn't spoken a word to Vince in years, and his leaving was a sore spot for the whole family. What would happen if Joe said he wanted to do the same thing?

 As a teen, Joe's nickname was Cosclilunghi, which means "long legs."

Luckily, Vince had just taken a step up in his career. A Pacific Coast League (PCL) team called the San Francisco Seals had just signed Vince to play right field. The PCL was basically the major league of the western states. It turned out heroes who were talked about from Seattle to San Diego, just like the Yankees, the Cubs, and the Red Sox turned out heroes in the East. Plus it had been a stepping-stone to the majors for a lot of local players. Vince had hit the big time. Once he was signed, Vince came home and dropped $1,500 on the table in front of his father—more money than Giuseppe had seen in his lifetime. It was a few months' salary plus Vince's signing bonus. From

17

that moment on, Giuseppe decided that playing ball for a living might not be such a bad idea.

❝ *My father wanted to know where he stole it.* **❞**

—JOE DIMAGGIO ON HIS DAD'S REACTION TO BROTHER
VINCE'S NEWFOUND RICHES AS A BASEBALL PLAYER

Joe was in the clear. But where to start? Once again, Vince stepped in to help his little brother. At the end of the 1932 season, the San Francisco Seals' shortstop decided to take an early vacation. Seals manager Ike Cavney was at a loss. Where was he supposed to find a shortstop to play the last few games of the season? Vince had a suggestion—his little brother Joe.

Joe was invited to Seals Stadium and warmed up with the team. Cavney decided he was good enough to give him a shot, and Joe played in the last three games of the season. He got a few hits and played well enough to earn himself an invitation to the Seals spring training in 1933. This was it. Joe's big break had come. Now all he had to do was make the team.

Chapter Three

A Major League Deal

Landing a spot on the San Francisco Seals in 1933 wasn't going to be easy, even for a talent like Joe DiMaggio. The country was in the middle of the Great Depression. After the stock market crash of 1929, people all over the country had lost their savings and their jobs. Many people didn't even have the money to feed their families, let alone buy a twenty-five-cent ticket to a baseball game. Much like other teams across the country, the Seals were feeling the strain. Attendance was down, so they didn't have the cash to pay a lot of extra players. They could only keep eighteen or nineteen players on their roster, and they already had twenty players returning from the year before, not to mention hundreds of wannabes. Joe knew that his chances of making the team were slim.

One of the returning players was Augie Galan, the shortstop who had taken his early vacation the year before. He was a rising star and a much better fielder than Joe. If Joe was going to make the team, he was going to make it based on his hitting. Of course, to show off his hitting, he had to get into a game, and early in spring training, it looked like that might never happen. Ike Cavney kept putting Galan in at shortstop, never giving Joe the chance to prove himself.

Then, in the last exhibition game of spring training, Galan got hurt, and Cavney put Joe in to replace him. Joe couldn't have been more excited. This was his chance! He had to show Cavney that he could play at short just as well as Augie could. He ran out onto the field . . . and proceeded to make four errors. Joe's fielding was bad and his throwing was even worse. Later, one of the reporters covering the game wrote that Joe looked "bewildered." It was a miserable performance.

❝*When I was trying to play shortstop for the San Francisco Seals, I made lots of errors, all on throws. The people sitting back of first base used to get up and run.*❞

—JOE DiMAGGIO

But when it came to hitting, Joe was a whole different player. He hit almost everything the pitcher threw at him. Even with his awful performance in the field, Joe was offered a contract. Thanks to the tight budget, the Seals had to cut many veteran players who had worked their way up to big salaries. Instead they hired a lot of rookies, paying them the minimum salary. The Seals' owner, Charlie Graham, knew that hitting like Joe's could win ball games and that he could pay Joe a rookie's salary to do it. Even though there was no place for Joe in the field, Graham wanted him on his team, simple as that. Joe's dreams were coming true.

Tom, Joe's elder brother, stepped in to help Joe negotiate his contract. He managed to get his brother's salary up to $225 a month, which was double what other rookies made. Plus Tom got Graham to throw in two brand-new business suits as a bonus, which Joe later said Tom kept for himself. It was a small price to pay for Tom's help in the salary talks. Joe was a professional, paid ballplayer.

Of course, once Joe was on the team, Ike Cavney needed to figure out what to do with him. He knew that Joe could be one of the great hitters of his time, so he decided to make his new rookie into a fielder as well. He taught Joe the finer points of playing shortstop to back up Augie Galan. He showed Joe how to stand like a shortstop, knees bent with a wide stance so he could get a jump on the ball whichever way it was hit. He taught him how to throw sidearm. But nothing helped much. Joe was thinking too hard. He wasn't a natural at short or at first base, where Cavney tried him next. Joe's manager was going to have to find a new position for him. But where?

In the third game of the season, during the ninth inning, Cavney told Joe to go out and play right field—his brother Vince's position. Vince was sitting the game out with a sore arm, and Cavney had Joe relieve Vince's replacement, just to see how he would do. Joe couldn't believe it. He'd never played out-field in his life, and the last thing he wanted was to try to take Vince's job. But Vince told him to get out there and Joe went. He didn't make a single play in that inning, but Vince was soon cut from the team in favor of Joe. Vince was injured, and the Seals needed Joe's hitting.

> During his first season as a Seal, Joe's last name was spelled DeMaggio because Joe didn't care enough to correct anyone.

Vince understood the decision. This was a business, after all. He went on to get a job with another PCL team, the Hollywood Stars. But Joe, while glad to be on the team, was depressed about losing his brother. He was only eighteen years old, and he was lonely without Vince, especially on the road. Still shy, Joe had a hard time making friends on the team, and without Vince, he had no one to talk to. Plus he had a new position to learn. The pressure was on.

Luckily, Joe turned out to be pretty good in the outfield. He had a strong arm that was perfect for rocketing balls in from far right. And he was fast, able to run down the ball wherever it was hit. It looked like he had finally found his place. Unfortunately, his hitting was going down the tubes.

Without his brother around, Joe wasn't only sad, he was slumping. His average was a lowly .250 in the month of April, and the Seals were losing game after game. The poor hitting continued through May, and Joe couldn't seem to bring himself out of it. Normally he would have been dropped from the team, but the Seals were doing so badly, they didn't even see the point. Then, for no apparent reason, everything suddenly turned around.

On May 28, Joe started hitting. He was hitting everything— doubles, triples, homers. He was hitting off pitchers that no one else could hit. Joe's teammates were amazed—and inspired. The more hits Joe racked up, the better the team played. They rallied around Joe, who became a bit of a sensation around the league. He went off on a hitting streak like they had never seen before. Attendance at the stadium doubled and kept climbing as the Seals started to win and Joe's hitting streak continued. Fans even turned out at away games to root for the Seals. Everyone wanted to see this rookie hit!

All throughout the streak, Joe seemed emotionless. He hardly ever smiled, even when he hit homers and the crowd went wild. He would simply duck his head, round the bases, and trot back into the dugout. His behavior earned him the nickname Dead Pan Joe from the *San Francisco Chronicle*. The kid just never looked excited.

But even if Joe was all business on the outside, inside he was beaming. He was proud of his performance, happy to have proved that he deserved his job. Most of all, he was relieved to be out of that inexplicable slump.

The hitting streak went on for sixty-one consecutive games, and by the end, Joe was a star. He finished the season with a .340 batting average—a far cry from that .250 he had early in the season. He even got his picture in *The Sporting News,* his favorite magazine. All over California, there were rumors that Joe would join the major leagues next season—that scouts were already checking him out. But if they were, they hadn't told Joe about it. At the end of the season, he went home to North Beach and his family, a local hero.

 Joe loved Superman comics and always knew when the next issue was coming out.

In 1934 Joe took the field for the Seals again and started out like gangbusters, hitting .370 in his first two months. The crowds loved him, but off the field, he was lonely. He still had a hard time making friends, and when the team was on the road, he kept mostly to himself, eating alone and spending most of his time reading *The Sporting News* in his hotel room. By this time, it was common knowledge that Joe was being watched by major league scouts. Everyone wanted this incredible hitter, and the New York Yankees in particular had an eye on him. This was a huge thing for Joe. The Yankees were the greatest team in baseball. Every ballplayer in the country wanted to play for them. He was on the verge of stardom.

"*Don't even think twice about it. This kid is ready for the major leagues—now.***"**
—SCOUT JOE DEVINE TO YANKEES GENERAL MANAGER
ED BARROW

And then on May 21, 1934, the dream came crashing down. Joe slipped getting out of a bus and twisted his knee badly. He took a few days off, hoping it would heal, but it didn't get any better. Still, Joe didn't want to lose his job, so he came back and tried to play. Throughout the summer, his perform-ance was iffy at best. He could hit, but then he would limp around the bases. He couldn't play right field because he couldn't run, so he ended up pinch hitting, but not all that well. Clearly Joe was in a lot of pain. Who knew if he would ever be the player he used to be? The scouts stopped paying attention. Joe was too much of a risk.

Still, the Yankees knew there had been something special about Joe. All he had to do was heal up and he could be that special again. They decided to take a chance on him. Joe was under contract with the Seals, so any team that wanted him would have to pay the Seals for him. Before the injury, rumor had it that Graham and the Seals could get as much as $75,000 for Joe. With his injury, the Yankees offered $25,000 plus five players. Charlie Graham snapped up the deal. Joe was damaged goods, and this was a great price for damaged goods.

❝[It was] the best deal I ever made.**❞**
> —ED BARROW ON TRADING FIVE PLAYERS
> PLUS $25,000 FOR JOE DIMAGGIO

The deal also included a bonus. Joe would stay in San Francisco for one more season and play with the Seals. This was good for the Yankees because it gave them a chance to see if Joe could come back without having to pay him a year's salary. If he stayed injured and couldn't play, they wouldn't lose anything more than the money they had already paid. It was good for the Seals because people in San Francisco and around the PCL still came out to the ballpark to see Joe, injured or not. The Seals would continue making ticket money off him in 1935.

For the time being, everyone would just have to sit back and wait. Would Joe recover and return to stardom, or would he succumb to the injury and just fade away?

Chapter Four

The Next Babe

In 1935 Joe proved that the Yankees were right to gamble on him. Under the coaching of his new manager, Francis "Lefty" O'Doul, Joe's fielding continued to improve and he learned how to hit homers down the left-field line—the shortest distance for a home run in Yankee Stadium. Lefty had played in the big leagues from 1919 through 1934, and he told Joe stories about what it was like to play in those huge stadiums against the greatest players in the world. Joe was enthralled. He couldn't wait to get to New York.

And it was becoming more and more clear that he would definitely get there. Joe's knee was healing nicely and he was making incredible plays in the field, running with great speed and making spectacular catches. Through the summer and into the fall, Joe's batting average hovered around the .400 mark, occasionally going *above* .400. For the first time in years, the Seals finished the season in first place and won the PCL championship in a playoff against the Los Angeles Angels. Joe finished the season with a stellar .398 batting average and came in second for the batting title, losing to Oscar Eckhardt, who hit .399. He had 34 home runs, 49 doubles, 18 triples, and 24 stolen bases.

The Yankee organization couldn't wait to get this young phenom to New York. After negotiating his salary with the help of Lefty and Lefty's friend, the legendary major leaguer Ty Cobb, Joe signed his contract with the Yankees. The New York newspapers made a huge deal out of Joe. Even in the East, fans and writers had heard all about Joe DiMaggio's amazing hitting. They saw him as a potential replacement for Babe Ruth, who had left the Yankees in 1934. The 1935 season was the third year in a row that the Yankees had come in second place for the pennant. The sportswriters said Joe could single-handedly turn the slumping Yankees around. One headline read, "Fans Expect Recruit from Coast to Be Cobb, Ruth, Jackson in One." Ty Cobb, Babe Ruth, and Travis Jackson were three of the greatest ballplayers who had ever lived. That was a lot of hero for Joe to live up to!

The fans were salivating to see Joe play. The press could hardly wait to get its hands on him. The pressure was on for this rookie not only to succeed, but to excel. The Yankees' general manager, Ed Barrow, was concerned that all the hype might get to Joe—that he might get shaken up by all the attention. So during spring training, Barrow met with Joe and told him not to pay too much attention to the insanity—not to get too worked up. Joe sat across from Barrow and said, "Don't worry, Mr. Barrow. I never get excited." He was still Dead Pan Joe.

❝ *Never before has a recruit fresh from the minors created the furor which DiMaggio has stirred up.* **❞**

—DAN DANIEL, SPORTSWRITER

For his part, Joe couldn't figure out why everyone was so eager to talk to him. He knew he was a good hitter, but he was just a kid from San Francisco. When he looked around at the Yankees' team, he saw real heroes like first baseman Lou Gehrig, the team captain, and the great pitcher Red Ruffing. Joe found it hard to believe that the press even knew he existed. He was in awe of the players around him, and he resolved to do his best on the field so they wouldn't think he was getting all this attention for nothing.

Joe's performance in his first spring training game proved he belonged in the major league. The Yankees put him in the lineup batting third—Babe Ruth's old spot. In his first at bat, Joe hit a line drive triple. Then he went on to hit three more singles.

In the next game, Joe got two more hits. By then, the word was out. Joe DiMaggio *was* as good as everyone was saying. People flocked to the ballpark, wanting to be among the first to see the new star play. In Joe's fourth game, he slid into second and a Boston Bees fielder stepped on his foot—hard. Joe played the rest of the game, but the next day his foot was swollen beyond belief.

Joe was devastated. The season hadn't even started yet, and he'd already gotten injured. But the team doctor told him there was nothing to worry about. He put Joe's foot in a diathermy machine, which was supposed to use heat to heal the swelling and pain.

During the treatment, Joe felt his foot getting hotter and hotter until it was extremely uncomfortable, but he didn't say anything. He figured the doctor knew what he was doing and knew how to work the machine. Unfortunately, Joe was wrong. The doctor left his foot in the machine too long, and Joe ended up with first-degree burns all over his foot. Joe missed the rest of spring training and the first three weeks of the season.

❝ *He was a little timid. He didn't bother anyone, and they didn't bother him.* **❞**

— MANAGER JOE MCCARTHY ON JOE DIMAGGIO'S
FIRST DAYS WITH THE YANKEES

The hype didn't die down, however. Even while Joe was recovering, the press kept talking about him, wondering when he would be back and psyching up the fans for his first performance. On the day of Joe's first regular season game as a Yankee, May 3, 1936, more than 25,000 fans showed up at Yankee Stadium, the largest crowd since opening day. They were all dying to see Joe hit, and they weren't disappointed.

In that first game, Joe hit two singles, a double, and a triple. The fans and the press gushed all over him. This was it! This was exactly what they needed to bring the Yankees back to glory! And it wasn't just the batting. Joe turned out to be stellar in the field as well, rocketing in balls from the far outfield and getting out runners who thought they would have no problem making it to base. By the end of May, Joe led the league with a .411 batting average and was the highest vote-getter for an American League All-Star outfielder. The fans were so crazy over him that he sometimes had to be escorted from the stadium by a team of police officers. Joe was a real celebrity. He was the young hero of New York.

But when the day of the All-Star game arrived, Joe was anything but a hero. In the All-Star game, a team made up of the best players from the American League (AL) plays a team made up of the best players from the National League (NL). Joe was the most famous rookie in the AL, and the fans couldn't wait to see him play. Unfortunately, Joe fell apart that day. He never hit safely, and he committed multiple errors in the field. Just as he had early in his Seals career, Joe seemed bewildered again. The NL went on to win their first ever All-Star game. It was only the fourth All-Star game ever played, but the AL had been very proud of their three-game winning streak. The end of that streak was blamed on one guy, Joe DiMaggio.

Joe was extremely frustrated by his awful play, but not nearly as frustrated as the press was. They ripped Joe apart, making headlines out of his embarrassing performance. Suddenly Joe learned how quickly all his friends in the press could turn into enemies. After that, if Joe made a mistake in a game, he would mope around the dugout. If the Yankees lost, he would blame himself. There was always something he could have done better, a ball he could have hit farther or a play he could have made faster. He would spend hours going over what had gone wrong. Joe DiMaggio was becoming a perfectionist. He was going to make the most of his career, no matter what it took.

> ❝I never guessed what pitch was coming no matter who was pitching. I always looked for a fastball, and if it was something else, I adjusted.❞
>
> —JOE DIMAGGIO

That summer, an accident on the field turned into a stroke of luck for Joe. He collided head-on with Myril Hoag, the center fielder, while they were both chasing after the same ball. Hoag was badly injured and had to sit out the rest of the season. The Yankees needed a center fielder, so manager Joe McCarthy moved Joe to center. Joe excelled at the position. The center field area was huge and it gave the fleet-footed Joe room to run and roam. He would be a center fielder for the rest of his career.

In Joe DiMaggio's day, baseball leagues didn't hold playoff games before the World Series. The AL team with the most wins during the regular season always faced off against the NL team with the most wins.

Joe's rookie season had been marked by ups and downs. The stellar beginning, the injury, the big hits, the awful All-Star game, and a new position on the team. Through it all, he managed to play like the pro he was, finishing the season with a .323 batting average, 29 home runs, and 125 runs batted in (RBIs). It was the best performance by a rookie in the entire league. He also did exactly what the Yankees and their fans wanted—he helped the team out of its hole. The Yankees clinched the AL pennant on September 9, the earliest clinch in history. They finished a whopping nineteen and a half games ahead of the second-place Detroit Tigers and would face the New York Giants in the World Series.

Joe was beside himself. It was his first season in the major leagues, and he was going to the World Series. All he could do was hope that he would play well and help his team. He wanted to prove to the world that his performance in the All-Star game was just a fluke.

In the first game of the series, the Yankees lost 6–1, falling victim to pitcher Carl Hubbell's infamous screwball. But in game two, they came back and won 18–4. All nine of the hitters in the Yankees lineup had at least one hit, and none of the five pitchers the Giants tried could do anything to stop them. The Yankees won again in game three but this time by a much tighter margin, 2–1. After game four, which the Yankees won 5–2 off a two-run homer by Lou Gehrig, it seemed that the Yankees would take the series easily. But the Giants came back in game five and won in extra innings, 5–4.

Going into the sixth game, the Yankees were up three games to two. One more win and the series would be theirs. In the top of the ninth inning of game six, the Yankees led by only one run. Anything could happen. Joe was on third base when his teammate Bill Dickey hit the ball toward first. Joe took off the second the bat hit the ball, running for home and hoping to put his team up by two. But the first baseman picked up the ball, stranding Joe between third and home. When the first baseman rocketed the ball toward third, Joe sprinted toward home. He knew this would be a tough play to make, but he had to score.

The third baseman threw the ball to the catcher, who caught it well before Joe reached home and crouched in Joe's way. It was going to be an easy out.

Well, it would have been an easy out if the runner had been anyone other than Joe DiMaggio. Instead of barreling into the catcher, Joe launched himself over the catcher's outstretched arm, twisted in the air, and landed *behind* the catcher with his hand on home plate. The catcher hadn't tagged Joe. He was safe!

The crowd went nuts over Joe's acrobatics. They couldn't believe what they had just seen. After that, the Yankees went on a hitting tear, scoring six more runs in that inning and making the final score 13–5. The Yankees had won the World Series in six games.

During his rookie season, Joe once hit two home runs in a single inning. He was the first Yankee ever to do so.

Joe had nine hits in the series and three RBIs, but it was that play that made him the hero of the season. Even the Giants manager, Bill Terry, recognized that the win was largely due to the rookie. "I've always heard that one player could make the difference between a losing team and winner and I never believed it," Terry said. "Now I know it's true."

Joe had excelled in his rookie season. He'd made himself a star and was going home a World Series champion. His career was off to an incredible start.

Chapter | Five

A New Star in Town

Joe was a big star when he returned to the family home in San Francisco that off-season. He brought his parents the $6,400 bonus he had earned by playing on the winning World Series team, and he bought his brother Mike a new fishing boat.

---

66 *I'm just a ballplayer with one ambition, and that is to give all I've got to help my ball club win.* **99**

—JOE DIMAGGIO

Joe spent the winter hanging out with his family, posing for pictures when reporters stopped by, and getting into shape for next season. All he wanted was to get in a full spring training this year. After last year's burned foot disappointment, he wanted to start the season in top form.

Unfortunately, Joe's plans didn't work out quite as he'd planned. After nine exhibition games in the preseason, Joe came down with tonsillitis and had to have his tonsils removed. He was out for three weeks of the season while he recovered from the surgery. Once again, Joe would miss opening day.

He returned on May 1, 1937, in a game against the Boston Red Sox, and it soon became clear that Joe's illness hadn't affected his game one bit. In fact, he started out the season hitting even better than he had the year before. Joe was committed to his game. On game days, he would get to the stadium at least an hour early, if not more, to warm up, hoping to keep up with those teammates who had gotten in a full preseason. His hard work paid off.

Over the summer Joe was hitting so many home runs that the press started to wonder if he could threaten Babe Ruth's single-season record of sixty homers. At the end of July, Joe had racked up thirty-one home runs, and on the last weekend of the month, he hit three total—including two in one game. Joe was on fire and the Yankees honored him by changing his jersey number from nine to five—the lowest number a player could have on the Yankees without taking a number from Yankee legends like Babe Ruth or Lou Gehrig, who was still with the team.

Joe's success extended beyond the ballpark as well. That summer he was asked to take a small part in a major motion picture, playing himself. Joe agreed, and it was on the set of the film, *Manhattan Merry Go Round*, that he met a young actress named Dorothy Arnold. The two were soon dating, and it seemed Joe would have as much good luck in love as he had in baseball.

After July, Joe's home run hitting slowed down and he ended the season with forty-six. He hadn't broken any records, but he had hit more homers than anyone else in either league—not too shabby a performance. His batting average was .346 for the season, and he was second in the league in hits and RBIs. Joe knew he had a shot at winning the Most Valuable Player (MVP) award, but he ended up losing by just four votes to Charlie Gehringer, a veteran player from Detroit who had won the batting crown with a .371 average. (The batting crown or batting title goes to the player in the league with the highest average for the season.)

Still, Joe wasn't too disappointed. As always, the team's performance was more important to him than his own records and awards. And the team was doing amazingly well. They won the pennant once again and met up with the New York Giants in the World Series for the second year in a row. For the second year in a row, they beat those Giants, this time four games to one. In the series Joe had six hits, including one home run, and four RBIs. The Yankees and Joe DiMaggio were champions once again.

Joe's father, Giuseppe, was in the stands to see Joe hit his first World Series homer in 1937.

Joe returned home for the winter, and this time he helped his big brother Tom start a new career. Together the two brothers opened a restaurant called Joe DiMaggio's Grotto, on Fisherman's Wharf in San Francisco. Joe's name would bring people in, and Tom's food would keep them there. The two brothers would split the profits of what soon became a booming business. Meanwhile, thanks to his salary and another World Series bonus, Joe was able to buy his family a new house with a garage, a yard, and all the trimmings. There was nothing Joe loved better than to use his success to help his family. Everything was going perfectly.

During the off-season, Joe began negotiations for his 1938 contract. Joe knew how much he had helped the Yankees over the last two seasons, and he decided it was time to cash in. He asked for a salary of $40,000, which was huge back in those days. Colonel Ruppert, the Yankees' owner, thought Joe was crazy. Lou Gehrig, the team's captain, who had played in more than two thousand consecutive games, made only $36,000 in 1937. Joe's response to this fact? He thought Lou was underpaid.

Joe refused to sign for anything less than the salary he felt he deserved, but the Yankees wouldn't cave. They were offering $25,000, which would make Joe the highest-paid third-year player in baseball, and they were sticking to it. The story of Joe's "greed" leaked to the press and they had a field day with it. Who did this young kid think he was, demanding more money than the legendary Lou Gehrig?

Joe was sure that the Yankees would realize how much they needed him and offer him more money. But soon spring training started, and there was still no offer from the Yankees. Even Joe McCarthy, the Yankees' manager and one of Joe's biggest fans, was quoted in the press saying they didn't need Joe. The season started with a Yankees loss and Joe still sitting in San Francisco. Finally, it seemed it was time to panic.

❝The Yankees can get along without DiMaggio. And that $25,000 is final.❞

—MANAGER JOE McCARTHY, SPEAKING ABOUT JOE'S SALARY DISPUTE IN 1938

On the third day of the season, Joe couldn't take it anymore. He didn't want to lose his job. He notified Colonel Ruppert that he'd accept the Yankees' offer. Ruppert told him to come to New York. The trouble was over.

Or was it? When Joe took the field for his first game, he was soundly booed by the crowd. All the fans thought he was nothing but a big greedy baby. He had missed opening day for the third year in a row and for what? Did he think he was better than the rest of the Yankees? Did he think he didn't *need* spring training? Please! New Yorkers didn't like guys who put themselves before the team, and they let Joe know it.

After that, Joe learned his lesson. He knew that the only way he could prove himself to the fans was by winning, so that was what he set out to do. Joe was all business, all about the game. His perfectionist attitude returned with a vengeance, and his teammates respected that. Sometime during the season, Joe, with his serious work ethic, became the symbolic leader of the team. He would lead the players out of the dugout onto the field, and he was always the last to come back in. When the Yankee captain, Lou Gehrig, started to slump midway through the season, Joe took over as cleanup hitter. He ended the season with a .324 average, 32 home runs, 140 RBIs, and only 21 strikeouts in 599 at bats. The Yankees, with their stellar pitching and impressive hitting, beat the Boston Red Sox to the pennant by nine and a half games.

The Yankees faced the Chicago Cubs in the World Series. They won the first two games at Chicago's Wrigley Field, taking the first by a score of 3–1, thanks to Red Ruffing's awesome pitching. In the second game, Frank Crosetti hit an eighth-inning homer that scored two runs and shocked the Cubs so badly they couldn't come back. Then Joe hit another in the ninth inning to seal the deal, and the Yanks won 6–3. The third and fourth games were played in Yankee Stadium, and the Yanks quickly put the Cubs away, sweeping the series in four games. The Yankees were on top of the world, and Joe wasn't getting booed anymore. The fans loved him once again.

In 1938 the Yankees earned the nickname "The Window Breakers" because so many of their home runs flew out of whatever park they were playing in and broke windows on nearby buildings.

In 1939 Joe didn't argue about his contract. Yankees owner Colonel Ruppert had passed away during the off-season, and Joe didn't want to do anything that might seem disrespectful. He had learned his lesson from the fans the year before. He accepted the same salary as he had been offered in 1938 and went to spring training ready to work.

This year, Joe made it to his first opening day, but six games into the season, he tore his calf muscle and was out once again. He took a month to recuperate and had a lot of time to think about what he wanted to do with his season. By the time he came back in June, he had decided. This year, he wanted to win the batting crown. Once he made up his mind, there was no stopping him.

Joe hit like crazy all through the summer. For most of the season, his average was an astounding .400—sometimes better. Meanwhile, he was also playing great in the field. It seemed like Joe somehow knew where the ball was going to be hit before it ever left the bat. Most of the time he was standing right under the ball far before it came to him. He was producing on defense as much as on offense.

Off the field, Joe was still dating Dorothy Arnold, and he decided that he wanted as much happiness and success off the field as he was having on the field. He asked Dorothy to marry him, and she said yes. Everything was falling into place for Joe.

Near season's end, Joe was far ahead of any other batter in the league. The batting crown was in his sights, as was a .400-plus season—a huge feat for a major league ballplayer. Then that fall, Joe developed an eye infection that prevented him from seeing out of his left eye—the eye that faced the pitcher when Joe was at bat. Obviously this affected his hitting, and Joe expected McCarthy to sit him out to help him keep his average above .400. McCarthy had other plans, however. He told Joe that he would look like a crybaby if he sat out games for an eye infection, and instead of resting his star, he kept putting him in the lineup. Joe's average dropped steadily, and he couldn't do anything about it.

Ty Cobb once advised Joe to soak his bats in olive oil, then let them dry for a couple of weeks. He claimed that it made the bats more springy.

Joe was angry with McCarthy, and when he finished the season with a .381 average, he blamed his manager for the disappointment. Still, a .381 was good enough to win the batting crown he had set out to claim. Joe had his title, and the Yankees had won the pennant once again, this time by seventeen games.

The Yankees would face the Cincinnati Reds in the 1939 World Series. Veteran pitcher Red Ruffing put the Reds away in game one with a 2–1 victory. The next day, Monte Pearson pitched a shutout for the Yanks and they won by a score of 4–0. In game three, the Reds managed to score three runs, but it wasn't enough to combat all the homers the Yankees produced. Charlie Keller hit a two-run homer in the first, Joe hit a two-run homer in the third, Keller hit *another* two-run homer in the fifth, and Bill Dickey hit a solo homer, also in the fifth. The Yankees trounced the Reds 7–3.

The Yankees were set up for another four-game sweep, but Reds pitcher Paul Derringer did everything he could to keep that from happening. Game four was a nail-biter, with the score still at 0–0 at the top of the seventh inning. Then things opened up. Keller and Dickey both hit solo homers, making the score 2–0. The Reds answered with four runs in the seventh and eighth. In the ninth inning, the Yankees tied it up when Bill Dickey batted in a run and then Joe beat a throw to the plate to score the fourth run. The game went into extra innings.

In the tenth, with a runner on first and one on third, Joe hit a single to right field and drove in a run. That would have been it, but the right fielder mishandled the ball and allowed Charlie Keller to head for home. The fielder fired the ball toward home plate, but the Reds catcher couldn't hold on to it and when Keller barreled into him, the ball rolled away. In all the confusion, Joe managed to round all the bases and head for home untouched.

The Yankees scored three runs on Joe's "single" and the Yankees won the game 7–4. The Yankees had swept their second consecutive World Series and won their fourth straight— becoming the first team in major league history to win four consecutive World Series. As an added bonus, Joe won the MVP award in a landslide. He and his team were both at the top of their game.

Chapter | Six

Joltin' Joe

As always, Joe spent his off-season with his family, but this year, it was a little different. On November 19, 1939, Joe married Dorothy Arnold at a ceremony in San Francisco. The event was more like a circus than a wedding. Fans packed the Church of Saints Peter and Paul and crowded onto the sidewalk and streets around it. They all wanted to get a glimpse of their hero on the biggest nonbaseball day of his life.

Joe hated all the attention. He believed a wedding should be about family and close friends. But he made it through the day and spent his off-season with his new bride and his family in San Francisco. His little brother, Dominic, had recently been recruited by the Boston Red Sox, so Dom and Joe spent a lot of time working out together, getting ready for the 1940 season.

As was becoming a pattern with Joe, he was injured again during spring training in 1940, this time wrenching his knee. He missed opening day once more, and by the time he came back, the Yankees were already proving this wouldn't be one of those exciting, stellar seasons their fans were used to. Some people blamed the slump on the ailing Yankee veteran Lou Gehrig, who had retired the year before after being diagnosed with amyotrophic lateral sclerosis (ALS). Fans thought the Yankees might be shaken over losing their once unstoppable captain—that the slump was all mental. Whatever it was, the Yankees, try as they might, never could catch up with the first-place Detroit Tigers. They came close but ended up finishing two games behind the Tigers and one game behind the Cleveland Indians. The mighty Yankees were in third. Their string of championships had finally been cut.

Joe won the batting crown again that year with a .352 average. He also had 31 home runs and 133 RBIs. But none of this was good enough for Joe. His team had lost, and that meant the season was a failure, no matter how good his personal numbers were. He and Dorothy headed back to San Francisco for the off-season. Joe was much more comfortable at home with his family. There he felt like he could regroup, figure out what had gone wrong, and start over.

After the Yankees' dismal season in 1940, a lot of Joe's teammates were cut from the roster. Thanks to his standout performance, winning the batting crown and leading the team,

Joe wasn't cut but was offered a raise. Even with this vote of confidence, however, Joe didn't feel like his job was secure. Many new faces greeted him at spring training. If the team didn't start out well, Joe had a feeling his job would be in jeopardy.

By the end of spring training, Joe had even more of an incentive to keep his job. He and Dorothy found out she was pregnant. Joe was ecstatic. With a growing family to support, he had to play his best.

66I don't think anyone can ever put into words the great things DiMaggio did. Of all the stars I've known, DiMaggio needed the least coaching.**99**

—JOE MCCARTHY

In 1941 Joe made it to opening day, for only the second time in his six-year career. But even with him in the lineup, the season started out badly. By early May, the Yankees were in third place. By the end of May, they were in fourth. It seemed like no one on the team knew how to hit anymore, including the two-time batting crown winner, Joe DiMaggio.

But then on May 15, Joe started off on his hitting streak and everything began to turn around. The more Joe hit, the more his teammates seemed to wake up. Suddenly they were hitting as well. In fact, during Joe's streak, the Yankees set a major league record of their own—a home run record. In twenty-five consecutive games, at least one Yankee hit a home run. The previous record had been set the year before by the Detroit Tigers at seventeen. You can bet that the Yankees felt good about busting the record of the team that had kept them from winning the pennant in 1940.

Amid all the excitement, Joe took a blow on June 2, 1941, when Lou Gehrig died. Lou was a huge star when Joe came to the Yankees, and Joe had always looked up to him, saying that Lou was the greatest Yankee of all time. Joe and the team were playing the Tigers in Detroit when Lou died. While McCarthy and Lou's best friend, Bill Dickey, flew back to New York for the funeral, Joe agreed to stay behind and lead the team. He hit a home run that day to honor the old slugger, but the Yankees lost 4–2.

Even in mourning, Joe continued his streak. By June 26, the Yankees were back in first place. The Yankees were like a whole new team. Instead of sighing and groaning in frustration, the fans were cheering. People showed up at ballparks all over the league, hoping to see DiMaggio continue his streak, excited to watch the revived Yankees.

Meanwhile World War II was raging in Europe and Asia. It seemed only a matter of time until the United States would be drawn into the fight. Evening radio programs were often inter-rupted for updates on the battles going on in Europe. But radio programs were also interrupted for updates on Joe's hitting streak. The streak distracted people from their war worries, and it gave them hope. Joe was a nationwide hero. A popular song-writer even composed a tune called "Joltin' Joe." It was a huge hit.

Owners of the other baseball clubs in the league were disappointed when Joe's streak came to an end. Thousands of people showed up at their parks whenever Joe was in town, hoping to see a little bit of history in the making. When the streak ended, attendance went down by half.

Joe took the major league record from George Sisler during that infamous doubleheader against Washington on June 29. "I'm glad a real hitter broke it," Sisler said. Then on July 2, Joe went for the all-time record in a home game against the Boston Red Sox, his brother Dominic's team. In fact, it was his little brother who almost robbed him of the record.

After failing to hit safely in his first at bat, Joe nailed one into center field on his second, a guaranteed extra-base hit. The crowd went wild, but someone out there in center was running for the ball like he was running for his life. The outfielder caught the ball at the last second, keeping Joe from his record for another at bat. The outfielder was Joe's little brother, Dom DiMaggio.

"It was one of the best [catches] Dom ever made," Joe said after the game. "But at that moment, the only thing on my mind was to withdraw the dinner invitation I had extended to my brother." In his next at bat, Joe hit a three-run homer, far out of the reach of his brother, and nabbed the record. When Joe broke the all-time record with his forty-fifth hit, the entire Yankees team streamed onto the field from the dugout to congratulate him. Joe McCarthy, the Yankees' manager, was in awe. "I don't believe anybody but a ballplayer is in a position to appreciate just what it means to hit safely in forty-five games," he said.

The streak had to end, of course, and it finally did on July 17, 1941, in a game against the Cleveland Indians. Joltin' Joe had racked up hits in fifty-six straight games. Joe said he would have liked to have beat his PCL record of sixty-one straight games, but at least the pressure was off. It was a typically understated Joe DiMaggio thing to say.

Even though the pitchers Al Smith and Jim Bagby stopped Joe on July 17, Joe went on to hit in his next sixteen games, making it seventy-two out of seventy-three games. Even more amazing, during the streak Joe had 223 at bats and only struck out in 7 of them.

The Yankees wrapped up the pennant in August, winning it by seventeen games. Ever superstitious, they waited until the pennant was a sure thing before throwing Joe a huge surprise party to celebrate the streak. Joe was humbled. When his teammates honored him, he knew for sure he had done something special.

When Joe's streak ended at fifty-six games, he lost a deal with the Heinz ketchup company. Their motto was "57 Varieties," and they had offered Joe a $10,000 endorsement deal if he extended his streak to fifty-seven.

The Yankees faced the Brooklyn Dodgers in the World Series. The Dodgers were counting on their great pitching to keep the Yankees' megahitters in line and give them the win, but it didn't quite work out that way. In game one, infielder Joe Gordon hit a two-run homer that gave the Yankees the lead in a 3–2 win. Red Ruffing showed some great pitching himself, holding the Dodgers to just six hits. In game two, it was the Yankees who went down, 3–2, letting the Dodgers tie the series at a game apiece. In game three, the Dodgers' pitching staff held the Bronx Bombers to only two runs, but it turned out to be enough as the Yankees won 2–1.

Then in the fourth game at Ebbets Field, things got really crazy. The Dodgers were winning in the top of the ninth inning, 4–3, and there were two outs. It looked like the Dodgers were going to tie the series. On a pitch to Tom Heinrich, Heinrich swung and missed for a third strike, but the Dodgers' catcher mishandled the ball, allowing Heinrich to dash to first. After that Joe came up and hit a single. Then Charlie Keller hit a double, scoring Heinrich and DiMaggio. Dickey walked, and Joe Gordon added to the lead with another two-run double. In the bottom of the inning, the Yankees' relief pitcher came in for three easy outs, and the Yankees won a wild one, 7–4. In game five, Heinrich hit a home run in the Yankees' 3–1 victory over the Dodgers. It had been a close series, and the Dodgers' pitchers *had* kept the Yankees' bats relatively quiet. But not quiet enough. Joe closed out his stellar year by winning the MVP award. He and the Yankees were back on top.

❝*You saw him standing out there and you knew you had a pretty darn good chance to win the baseball game.*❞
—Yankees pitcher Red Ruffing on Joe DiMaggio

In the off-season, Joe marked yet another success when his son, Joe Junior, was born on October 23, 1941. Playing the proud papa, Joe rushed around with cigars for his teammates and friends and posed with the baby for the press. Joe was such a huge star that even his baby was big news.

That spring Joe was surprised when he wasn't offered more money by the Yankee management. He figured his streak and the World Series win merited a reward. He asked the Yankees for a huge raise—from $37,500 to $80,000. The only player to ever earn that much in one season was the legendary Babe Ruth. Any other year, the Yankees might have considered giving up the cash for their star, but in December 1941, the United States had officially entered World War II. American boys were being shipped out to Europe and Asia, fighting for freedom and getting paid peanuts to do it. No one wanted to hear about a greedy star who wanted thousands to play a game, especially not fans with sons and brothers, husbands and fathers overseas.

Joe ended up settling for $42,500, but the press made a big deal of his salary dispute, and again he was booed at the ballparks. The Yankees played well, but all the negative attention got to Joe. His hitting was inconsistent, and the worse he played, the louder the boos grew. Many ballplayers, including Yankees Red Ruffing and Tom Heinrich, had enlisted to fight in the war, giving up their dream jobs as baseball players to fight for their country. There was pressure for Joe, who was hitting only .257, to go as well. The fans thought he wasn't living up to the money he wanted *or* the money he was getting. They wanted to know why Joe thought he was too good to fight with their boys. Dorothy started urging Joe to enlist as well.

Joe hated the image that he was some kind of greedy guy and a bad American. He made it through the summer and started hitting again, finishing the season with a .305 average. It was better than that .257 but still the worst of his career. He did have 21 home runs and 114 RBIs, but the fans were never quite on his side. It was a depressing year for Joe, capped off by an awful loss in the World Series to the underdog St. Louis Cardinals. Joe had only seven hits in the series, all of them singles.

Under pressure from the fans and his wife, Joe enlisted in the U.S. Army on February 17, 1943. A new and unexpected chapter of his life was about to begin.

Chapter Seven

In the Army Now

Joe DiMaggio took quickly to the army lifestyle. He was a hard worker and had always been very disciplined, plus he had natural leadership ability. These were all qualities valued in a good soldier. But after basic training, it became clear that Joe's life in the service wouldn't be just like that of any other private. Joe was a baseball star, and in the army, that meant he'd have a few special duties.

For his first year as a soldier, Joe was stationed in Santa Ana, California, where he and many of his former teammates and rivals from the major leagues were fashioned into a new baseball team. Brigadier General William Flood, one of Joe's commanding officers, was a huge baseball fan and didn't want to let all the talent the army had go to waste. And what talent he had! Red Ruffing was there, as was Mike McCormick of the Cincinnati Reds and Gerry Priddy of the Washington Senators.

Joe DiMaggio played with the San Francisco Seals from 1932 to 1935.

Joe poses with his mother, Rosalie, in 1936, his first year with the New York Yankees.

Baseball seemed to run in the DiMaggio family. Joe *(center)* is shown with Vince *(left)*, a member of the Cincinnati Reds, and Dominic *(right)*, outfielder for the Boston Red Sox.

In 1937 these four outstanding Yankee sluggers helped bring the team its second World Series win in a row. From left to right, they are Lou Gehrig, Joe, Bill Dickey, and George Selkirk.

On July 16, 1941, Joe set a record by getting at least one hit in fifty-six consecutive games.

Joe slides into home plate with the winning run in game four of the 1941 World Series, played against the Brooklyn Dodgers.

Joe's time in the army didn't keep him from playing baseball. He stands with *(left to right)* Vice Admiral Robert L. Ghormley, former Dodgers shortstop Pee Wee Reese, and Brigadier General William J. Flood.

Marilyn Monroe and Joe on their wedding day, January 14, 1954

Joe stands alongside Mickey Mantle *(center)* and Casey Stengel *(right)* at an Old Timers Day game in 1971.

George Turbeville, one of the team's pitchers, had pitched Joe his first-ever home run ball back in 1936. Together this all-pro team played squads from other branches of the military service, as well as local California teams. Even in fatigues, Joe found that his number-one skill was hitting a baseball. And his accomplishments still made headlines. His first home run as an army man was covered by the Associated Press, and the story was picked up by papers across the country.

When Joe joined the army, he was making $43,500 a year from the Yankees. His monthly salary in the service was $50.

Eight months after Joe enlisted, Dorothy filed for divorce. The two had grown apart, and even though they were both living in California, Dorothy felt she didn't see enough of her husband. Joe didn't know what to do. He didn't want his marriage to fail, but Dorothy seemed determined to end things. The divorce went through in May 1944.

A month later, the army sent Joe's unit to Hawaii. They shipped out on a huge battleship, and while his teammates and fellow soldiers enjoyed the trip, playing cards and hanging out on deck, Joe grew depressed. His marriage was over. Every move the army made for him seemed to take him farther and farther from his home and the baseball team he loved. Plus he knew that going to Hawaii meant he was one step closer to the fighting in Japan. Like many young soldiers on the brink of going into battle, Joe was afraid.

The soldiers didn't have much to do in Hawaii but sit around, play cards, and wait for their next orders. While Joe's fellow soldiers soaked up the sun, Joe became more and more frustrated. What was he doing here? He was missing out on the prime of his career and for what? To get paid next to nothing and sit around being bored all day? It didn't make sense to him. He missed the Yankees. He missed the crowds. He felt like he was losing out on his glory days.

From 1940 to 1946, Joe, Dom, and Vince were all major leaguers (though both Joe and Dom took 1943–1945 off to fight in World War II). Dom played for the Red Sox and Vince for the Pirates, Phillies, and Giants.

Dorothy, meanwhile, had moved back to New York with Joe Jr. That gave Joe one more reason to wish he was back in the Big Apple. His family was there—the family he wanted so desperately to win back.

All this sitting around and worrying finally got to Joe. In the fall of 1944, he developed a painful stomach ulcer. The doctors couldn't seem to do anything to treat it, and throughout the rest of the year, Joe was in and out of the hospital with stomach pain. He grew weak and thin because he could hardly bear to eat. When Joe's unit was shipped off to Guam, another step closer to battle, Joe convinced the army that he was too sick to fight. They sent him to a hospital in California to heal. He would rejoin his unit when he was healthy.

The Yankees won the World Series in 1943, their first year without Joe. But they wouldn't return to the series again until 1947.

But he never got healthy. Eventually, the army decided to move Joe again, and this time, he requested that they send him to a base in Atlantic City, New Jersey. Not only was it closer to Dorothy and Joe, but it just happened to be the city in which the Yankees would be holding spring training that year. Joe arrived on the East Coast in February 1945 and spent the next six weeks working to get his strength back. In August the army sent Joe to yet another army hospital, this one in St. Petersburg, Florida, which turned out to be the final stop on his unusual tour of duty. In September Joe was finally granted a medical discharge and released from duty. His ulcers had kept him from ever facing battle.

Joe immediately returned to New York but opted not to try to join the Yankees so late in the season. Instead he concentrated on winning Dorothy back. He did attend a few games at Yankee Stadium with Dorothy, much to the delight of the fans. After many late night phone calls and bouquets of flowers, Dorothy finally agreed to give Joe a second chance.

Meanwhile, the Yankees, who were under new ownership, offered Joe a new and pricey contract for the 1946 season. Joe signed with the team in November and was ecstatic. After three years of misery, he was back.

In his book *Few and Chosen*, legendary Yankee pitcher Whitey Ford named Joe DiMaggio as the best center fielder ever to play for the Yankees.

Dorothy decided to stay in New York and set up house for her family while Joe went off to spring training in 1946. Joe returned to the Yankees a new man. He was so happy to have his life back that he was actually talkative for the first time in his career. He chatted with the press, joked with his teammates, and walked around with a permanent smile on his face. Everyone was pleasantly surprised. They barely recognized this happy-go-lucky guy. Joe had been given a second chance, both with the Yankees and with Dorothy, and he knew it. He was determined to enjoy himself.

"I'm tired of being called a sourpuss. I'm learning to take all that stuff, and I guess maybe, if I could relax and smile a little more, it would be better all around," Joe said.

As a member of the Yankees, Joe earned the nickname "The Yankee Clipper" because he was fast like a clipper ship.

The new owners decided to get their team working early, and in February, they took the Yankees to a pre-spring-training camp in Cuba. It was the first time any major league team had left U.S. soil to train, and a lot of the players and coaches thought it was insane. Joe was pleased, however. He liked the idea of seeing a new place and *loved* the idea of getting a head start on training.

Joe and the Yankees were fantastic both in Cuba and after they got back to the United States. It seemed like these returning players had never left the game. Joe returned to New York to begin the season, flying high. He was going to rejoin Dorothy and Joe Jr. and remarry his bride. He was going to take New York by storm and return to his former glory. Everything was going his way.

But when Joe got back to New York, he found out that Dorothy had not, in fact, set up house for him. While he was away at spring training, she had fallen for someone else, and she was engaged. Just like that, Joe's hopes came crashing down around him.

Chapter Eight

Back in the Game

Joe had been hoping that the 1946 season would mark his triumphant return to baseball, but it didn't turn out that way. Events seemed to conspire against him. Not only had Dorothy left him, for good this time, but his closest friend on the team, Lefty Gomez, a veteran pitcher who had been Joe's roommate on road trips, retired. Plus Joe's manager, Joe McCarthy, was having a very bad year.

McCarthy was an old-school baseball man with traditional values. He wasn't interested in making any changes to the game. But the new ownership had other ideas. One of the new owners, Larry MacPhail, got under McCarthy's skin in a big way. MacPhail had been responsible for introducing night games in Cincinnati a couple of years back. Plus it had been MacPhail's idea to take the Yankees to Cuba, of all places. These new ideas didn't sit well with McCarthy, and the two clashed. Two months into the season, McCarthy couldn't take it anymore and quit. Joe had lost his wife, his friend, and his manager all in the course of two months. Not surprisingly, he went into a major slump.

In June Joe injured his left leg sliding into second base. He missed the All-Star game, and for the rest of the season his play was spotty. More injuries followed, including a heel spur (an abnormal growth on the heel bone) that would nag him for the second half of the season. In pain and unable to produce on the field, Joe grew frustrated and stopped talking to the press and to his teammates. He spent more and more time by himself, going over the team's losses, trying to figure out what had gone wrong. The old Joe was back. Unfortunately, the old Joe's hitting was not.

The Yankees finished a whopping seventeen games behind the first-place Red Sox. It was Joe's worst year ever, with a batting average of just .290 and only 25 home runs. That would have been a lot of homers for most players, but it wasn't good enough for Joe.

Then, to make matters worse, MacPhail tried to trade Joe to the Washington Senators in the off-season. The Yankees were trying to get rid of Joltin' Joe DiMaggio? That was unheard of! But even more unheard of was the fact that the Senators actually turned the offer down. They didn't even want Joe. The sheen was gone from DiMaggio's star.

Joe had surgery on that nagging left heel in the off-season, hoping to be in top shape when he returned to spring training in 1947. Unfortunately, his streak of bad luck continued. The doctors messed up the surgery, and Joe's heel became infected. It swelled up and was extremely painful. Instead of coming to spring training healthy, Joe showed up with a walking cane.

The Yankees sent Joe up north for *another* operation on his heel. This time the doctors fixed him up, but they told Joe he wouldn't be able to play until June or July. Joe couldn't believe it. He would miss *another* opening day. He lay in his hospital bed, worrying about his future. What if he didn't come back this year? What if this was really it for Joltin' Joe?

Well, Joe decided he wouldn't let this be the end. June or July wasn't good enough. He was going to get back to his team, and he was going to show the world that he was still a top player. He ordered a special shoe to cushion his heel and started running every day, trying to keep in shape. Joe was in the dugout soon enough, and five games into the season, he convinced his new manager, Bucky Harris, to put him into the lineup. Harris was young and green, and there was no way he was going to turn a veteran star like DiMaggio down. He sent Joe in. Joe thanked him by hitting a three-run homer.

Joe was the oldest Yankee on the team, and the rookies and other players looked up to him like the star he was.

Whatever Joe said was done. Whenever he spoke, they listened. Joe had come to the Yankees at a time when perfectionists like Lou Gehrig and Red Ruffing ruled the clubhouse. Those players accepted no mistakes. Joe preached that lesson to the next generation. They learned quickly how angry and disappointed Joe would get if the team lost. No one wanted to be the guy who put Joe in that mood.

---

66 *[Joe] had the greatest instinct of any ballplayer I ever saw. He made the rest of them look like plumbers.* 99

—Art Passarella, major league umpire

Rallying around Joe, the Yankees took first place in June and never looked back. They won nineteen straight games from June 19 to July 17, which hadn't been done since 1906, when the Chicago Cubs hit that mark. For the first time in years, it wasn't the Yankees' bats that were producing wins—no player on the team reached 100 RBIs that season—but the stellar pitching. Still, Joe contributed hugely with a .315 average, 20 home runs, and 97 RBIs. On September 15, the Yankees clinched the pennant and finished twelve games ahead of the second-place Detroit Tigers. Joe had made it clear early on that he wouldn't accept second best. His team had delivered for him.

That year the Yankees faced the Brooklyn Dodgers in the World Series. It was the first-ever televised series and neither team disappointed, dragging the dramatic contest out over seven games. Game one took place in Yankee Stadium, where the Yanks started off with a 5–3 win. After a 10–3 trouncing by the Yanks in game two, it looked like the good old days were back—that the Yankees might sweep. But not if the Dodgers had anything to say about it.

Game three was played at Ebbets Field, and the Dodgers got on the board early and big, scoring six runs in the second inning. Joe did everything he could to help the Yankees come back by hitting a two-run homer in the fifth, but it wasn't enough. His teammates contributed more runs throughout the game, but they still lost a tight one, 9–8. Just to add to the drama, in the fourth game, Yankees pitcher Bill Bevens almost pitched the first-ever World Series no-hitter. Unfortunately, the last batter in the ninth inning managed to get a hit and ended up winning the game for the Dodgers. The final score was 3–2.

In game five, the Yankees came back from the game four heartbreaker and won another close one, 2–1. Then in game six, the Dodgers were holding on to an 8–5 lead when Joe came to bat in the sixth. There were two men on base, and Joe knew that a hit would really help his team, while a homer would tie the game. Joe saw a good pitch and swung—whack!—rocketing the ball over left field. It looked like a homer for sure and Joe started to trot to first base, but at the last second, the Dodgers' left fielder jumped up and snatched the ball before it could go over the fence. There went the perfect homer and with it any chance for the Yankees to win. The World Series was tied at three games apiece.

Game seven was played in Yankee Stadium with Spec Shea as the Yankees' starting pitcher. He gave up two runs in the first two innings and was pulled from the game. It looked like the Dodgers might pull out a win, but the Yankees' relief pitcher, Joe Page, didn't allow a single run for five innings. The Yankees offense rallied around him, scoring five runs. The Yankees had won another World Series!

 In his thirteen-year-long career, Joe had only 369 strikeouts in 6,821 at bats.

Joe didn't have a single hit in that seventh game, but it was fine by him. He would have liked to have contributed, but all that mattered was that the Yankees had won. They had come back from their abysmal 1946 season and were world champions yet again.

Besides, Joe's teammates knew who had gotten them there. After the game, the victorious pitcher, Joe Page, who had allowed only one hit in five innings, said he did it all for Joe DiMaggio.

As the 1948 season began, Joe received his first raise since before the war. His salary was upped to $70,000 a year, a sign that the Yankees had every confidence in their star. In the first game of the season, Joe proved that they were right to count on him. He hit a long, powerful home run and threw a runner out at third from center field. Joe's hitting and his fielding were right on track. "I'm looking forward to a fine year. One of my best," Joe told reporters. Joe DiMaggio never came out and said things like that. The Yankees and their fans felt they were in for something special.

Unfortunately, it seemed Joe should have kept up the silent act. After his amazing debut, Joe was plagued by injuries. He'd had an operation on his elbow in the off-season, but his arm was still bothering him. Then, early in the summer, his right heel started to hurt, joining his left to make every step painful. Joe had to start wearing padded shoes so that he could run the bases and make plays. A lesser player might have sat out a few games, but Joe refused. Four teams were vying for first place, and he had to do his part.

His part, however, was smaller and smaller. His hitting grew inconsistent as the season wore on. Back in 1941, fans always knew that Joe was going to hit—that when he came to the plate, he could change the game. In 1948 they never knew which Joe they were going to see. Some days he would slam those huge home runs into the stands. Other days he couldn't seem to hit a thing. Joe didn't understand it. He wasn't doing anything differently. Why couldn't he seem to connect with the ball?

In a game in July 1948, a six-year-old boy somehow got onto the field at Yankee Stadium and ran right over to Joe with a pad and pen, asking for an autograph. The whole stadium watched in silence to see what Joe would do. He signed the autograph and sent the kid back to his parents, to the delight of the crowd.

Joe started spending extra hours at batting practice, taking pitch after pitch. He would stay up nights and practice his swing in front of the mirror, watching for glitches, checking to see if he was slowing down. He was obsessed with getting back into form. Joe DiMaggio wasn't anything unless he was helping his team win.

But things just got worse. All summer, his legs were killing him. Between the operations and all the sliding into bases, Joe was in constant pain. Often he could be seen limping off the field after long innings. By the end of the season, his right heel was causing shooting pains up his leg, and he was taking painkillers to try to dull the discomfort. To make matters worse, the Yankees couldn't pull it together, and they finished in third place. Joe's final numbers for the 1948 season were impressive. He had a .320 batting average, 39 home runs, and 155 RBIs. The home run total was his highest since 1937. Still, Joe hadn't lived up to his predictions. The Yankees were back in the gutter, and Joe was left wondering if his body was calling it quits.

After leading the team straight from first place to third, Bucky Harris was fired and the Yankees hired a new manager— Casey Stengel. Neither the press nor the players could figure out why the Yankee management felt this was the man to lead them back to glory. Stengel was a manager with a losing record and a reputation for being kind of goofy. This wasn't a guy Joe DiMaggio could respect, but there wasn't much he could do about it. He might be a star, but he knew his place, and he wasn't in charge. He was just going to have to deal with Stengel when the time came.

---

66 *He's bewildering. He doesn't seem to know what it's all about.* 99

—JOE DIMAGGIO ON HIS NEW MANAGER, CASEY STENGEL

Meanwhile, Joe had other problems on his mind. He had a second operation on his heel, this time a successful one. He was in good shape when he returned to spring training before the 1949 season, but it didn't last long. Stengel, eager to put to rest the rumors that he was some clueless moron, gave his players extra workouts to do on their first day. Wanting to prove he could keep up, Joe did everything that was asked of him, but it took its toll. The next day, he could barely walk.

Stengel went easier on his big star after that, but the damage was done. Joe was hurting all over, and his skills suffered because of it. In April Joe's heel started to swell, and the pain was excruciating. He consulted his doctors, who found another infection. Joe had to be hospitalized immediately. They said it would be weeks before his heel was healthy again. In fact, for two months after his release from the hospital, he could barely leave his hotel room. Forced to listen to his team on the radio, playing and winning without him (the Yankees were in first place), Joe fell into a deep depression. It was so bad that his friends had to come by just to make sure he was eating. Joe didn't know what to do with himself. He could barely walk. He certainly couldn't work out or play with his team, who didn't seem to need him anyway. What was the point?

Then in May, Joe's father passed away, and he had to fly back to San Francisco for the funeral. Joe was in so much pain he couldn't even help carry his beloved father's casket, which made him feel awful. He flew back to New York as soon as he could and continued his doctor-ordered bed rest. He was starting to wonder if it was ever going to end.

One day in June, Joe woke up and the pain in his heel was gone. He could hardly believe it. Just like that, everything had changed. He was so happy he felt like he could fly. He didn't want to move too fast and risk hurting himself again, so on June 27, he tested it out by playing in a charity game against the New York Giants. Joe didn't play particularly well. After all, he was out of practice and had barely moved for the past two months, but that wasn't the point. The point was, there was no pain. Joe DiMaggio was back!

> Joe had amazing eyesight, which he said helped him see what kinds of pitches were coming over the plate.

On June 28, Joe joined the Yankees in Boston to play in his first real game of the season, against the Red Sox. No one knew what to expect when Joe stepped to the plate, but he soon showed them. He hit a single and a home run in the game, plus he caught the winning out. Joe's teammates were stunned, but they couldn't have been happier. Their veteran and hero was back in top form. Joe went on to help them win the next two games against Boston, sweeping the three-game series. All the press could talk about was the big star's major comeback.

Joe played just as well throughout the summer, helping to keep his team on top. Then in the fall, bad luck struck again. Joe caught a nasty flu bug that landed him back in the hospital. He was still in his hospital bed in September when the Red Sox came back and stole first place from the Yankees. Joe was frustrated, but this time there was really nothing he could do about it. He was losing weight, and he was too weak to leave the ward. The Yankees would have to try to fight back without him.

On October 1, the Yankees planned to hold Joe DiMaggio Day. The festivities would include a pregame ceremony for their veteran star before the team took the field against the rival Red Sox. But up until the last minute, no one knew if Joe would even be able to get out of bed and make it to the ballpark. This was one day at the stadium, however, that Joe wasn't going to miss. He had lost eighteen pounds and he was exhausted, but he managed to drag himself out of bed to attend the ceremony. His mother was there, as was his brother Dominic, who was still playing for the Red Sox. Joe could barely stand as he was showered with gifts and accolades. When the ceremony was over, he was expected to speak, but he was so tired, he had to keep it short. In his speech, he thanked his managers and the fans, then finished with a few words that would go down in history. "I'd like to thank the good Lord for making me a Yankee," Joe said. Then he broke down in tears from all the emotion and exhaustion.

Joe's famous line from his 1948 speech was later painted on the wall above the tunnel leading from the home locker room to the dugout at Yankee Stadium. It's still there today.

Despite his illness, Joe took the field that day in a big win against the Red Sox. The Yankees were tied with their rivals for first place. Dog-tired and emotionally wrecked, all Joe could say about the win was, "Let's win tomorrow." Even with everything going on, his illness and his honors, Joe was focused on one thing—the pennant.

The next day the Yankees would face the Red Sox again in a winner-takes-all matchup. Joe knew that he could make or break the season for his team, so when he messed up an easy play in the ninth inning and the Red Sox were threatening to come back, he took himself out of the game. Joe wasn't a quitter, but he knew what to do to help his team. He wouldn't let his illness be the reason for their downfall. The Yankees went on to win the game 5–3, and the Yankees took the pennant from the Red Sox' grasp.

The Yankees went on to play the Brooklyn Dodgers in the World Series, where they won, four games to one. Joe was only two for eighteen at the plate, but one of those two was a home run in the last game. It reminded everyone—his teammates, the Yankees owners, the fans, and the Dodgers—that he wasn't done yet.

He was, however, exhausted. When the season was over, Joe went back home to San Francisco to stay with his family and rest.

Chapter Nine

Lucky to Be a Yankee

As the 1950 season opened, Joe was feeling good. He had recovered from his illness by spending the entire winter in San Francisco with his family and eating his mother's home cooking. His weight was back to normal, and he had regained his strength. There was no keeping him from training camp this year, where he actually stayed healthy. Joe was even in the lineup on opening day, a feat he had rarely accomplished in his twelve years in the major leagues.

In 1950 *The Sporting News* polled all major leaguers, asking which player they admired most. More than 85 percent said Joe DiMaggio.

The first game of the season was played at Fenway Park against his brother's Boston Red Sox. Joe looked as healthy as a rookie. He was all over the park making catches, and at the plate he hit a single, a double, and a triple. The press was psyched. Everyone was talking about how Joltin' Joe was back in top form.

Unfortunately, it didn't last. Joe was energized for that first game, but soon his injuries started to plague him again. His batting average for the first six weeks of the season was a meager .243.

The Yankees were scrambling to stay in first place and hold on to their title. Casey Stengel realized he was going to need more hitting. The only big hitters he had, however, were outfielders who weren't currently in the starting lineup. So Stengel made a move that stunned everyone—he moved Joe DiMaggio to first base so he could put a big hitter in center field.

The team, the press, and everyone who knew anything about the Yankees were floored. Joe was a veteran, a star. He played center field like he owned it. He had been there so long it seemed he *did* own it. This move was like a slap in the face to the most revered man on the team. Joe couldn't believe it. He hadn't played first base in years, since trying it out briefly with the San Francisco Seals. In fact, he joked about the move with the press. "Just tell me where first base is and I'm ready," he said. He might have been laughing on the outside, but inside, he was furious. Players like him should never be treated this way.

But responsible men like Joe also did what they were told and went where their managers felt they were needed. So on July 3, Joe played a full game at first base. He was awkward at the position, overthinking every play, and it was an unsuccessful experiment. Luckily for Joe, and maybe for Stengel, Joe's center field replacement, Hank Bauer, was injured during the game, and the next day, Joe was sent back to his old position.

It wouldn't be the last insult of the season, however. As Joe's hitting continued to decline, Stengel bumped him from the cleanup position to fifth in the batting order. Then on August 11, Joe DiMaggio was benched for the first time ever, in favor of the younger Hank Bauer. Joe might have deserved it—he had hit only four times in his last thirty-eight at bats—but Joe was still angry and the fans were shocked. This was their hero—their star—and he was riding the bench. Was Joe DiMaggio's career coming to an end?

66_There's no snap in my swing. I know what's wrong, but there's nothing I can do about it._**99**

—JOE DIMAGGIO

It was all the press could talk about. Would Joe retire at the end of the season? Had his body given out on him? The more

Joe heard about his impending retirement, the less he liked it. He only sat out six games before Bauer was hurt again. Stengel looked to Joe to take up his old spot, and Joe came back with a vengeance.

He started hitting again, and as always, when Joe was hitting, the Yankees came alive. They were in second place when Joe was benched, but soon after his return, they came back hard and stole first place from Detroit. Then in September, Joe had people recalling his 1941 hitting streak when he hit safely in nineteen straight games.

His average was climbing steadily, and at the end of this streak, he had bumped it up into the .280s. But that still wasn't good enough for Joe. He felt that anyone batting under .300 didn't belong in the big leagues. He had to keep working.

❝There is always some kid who may be seeing me for the first or last time. I owe him my best.❞

—JOE DiMAGGIO

And that he did. During the last six weeks of the season, Joe went on a hitting spree that gave him an average of .376 for those six weeks. It brought his final average up to .301—just above his own mental cutoff. It wasn't great, but maybe he was still good enough to stick around. Even better, the Yankees won the pennant and were headed to the World Series once again.

Batting fourth in the World Series, just after an up-and-coming catcher named Yogi Berra, Joe was hitless in the first game, whacked a home run in the second, and had one hit in the third. The Yankees won all three of those games. In game four, with the chance to sweep the Philadelphia Phillies, Stengel sent in rookie pitcher Whitey Ford. Ford had a shutout all the way into the ninth inning, when Philadelphia finally managed to score two runs. Still, it wasn't enough. Thanks to Ford, plus some stellar hitting by Berra, DiMaggio, and their teammates, the Yankees won and swept the World Series. It was a great performance and another victory, but Joe was worn out and exhausted by the end of the season. He even told a few reporters he might not come back.

That summer Joe and his family had found out that Joe's mother had cancer. As much as Joe loved his mother, he couldn't handle the misery and the pressure of being at home. Instead of staying in San Francisco, he answered any doubts the press had about another year and signed a new contract with the Yankees, who were more than happy to have their star return. "I'm out to surprise those who believe I am finishing up my career," Joe said.

Still, it seemed that Stengel and the Yankees were preparing for the day when Joe would be done. In 1949 they had scouted a young kid from Oklahoma named Mickey Mantle. Mickey was just nineteen, but he could hit like a pro and he was fast. He tore up the minor leagues in 1950 with a .383 batting average. He came to spring training with the Yankees, and he was all the press could talk about. Rumor had it that Mickey was being groomed to take over center when Joe retired.

Ever proud, Joe didn't want to seem like he was being pushed out of his spot on the team, so he gathered a few reporters together and told them this would be his last season. This was his decision, no one else's. Fortunately, Joe didn't have to spend the entire season wondering when Stengel would take him out of the game in favor of his new star. It became clear early on that Mantle couldn't handle the pressure of being a New York phenomenon as well as Joe had when he was a rookie. He choked in his first few games and was soon sent back to the minors in Kansas City to get his head straight. Joe was the undisputed center fielder once again.

But early in the season, Joe's many injuries and his aging body started to get to him. He sat himself out of a few games through May and June, when he knew he was too stiff or in too much pain to contribute. On June 17, Joe got word that his mother had slipped into a coma. He took the first flight out to San Francisco to be with her when she died. Upon his return, Joe was depressed and hurting. His fielding grew steadily worse.

On July 6, Joe was playing slow and stiff, and Casey Stengel didn't want to wait for the star to sit himself. In the middle of an inning, Stengel sent in another player, Johnny Hopp, to relieve the center fielder. Joe was livid. He was a star and a veteran and he couldn't be publicly humiliated like that. He told Hopp to get off the field and tell Stengel he would come out when he was ready. Things had already been strained between Joe and his manager, but after this episode, they were downright awful. Joe and Stengel wouldn't speak to each other for the rest of the season. Joe got messages from his manager through other players and barely ever responded. He grew more depressed and his playing more inconsistent.

Still, at the end of the season, when every game counts, Joe contributed big time. On September 16, he hit a two-run triple against the Cleveland Indians to help the Yanks to a tie for first in the AL. The next day, he scored the winning run to put the Yankees on top of the heap. Then on September 28, the Yankees had to defeat the Boston Red Sox in both games of a double-header to beat them to the pennant. They won the first game 8–0. Then in the second, it was Joe's three-run home run that gave the Yankees the win. Thanks to Joe, the team was on its way to another World Series.

The Yankees played the 1951 series against the New York Giants. Joe knew it would be his last. His body just couldn't take this anymore. After this championship, it would be time to hang up the spikes.

> ❝*I feel that I have reached the stage where I can no longer produce for my ball club, my manager, my teammates, and my fans the sort of baseball their loyalty to me deserves.*❞
>
> —JOE DIMAGGIO IN 1951

Joe wanted to go out with a bang, but early on in the series, it looked like that wouldn't happen. Joe failed to hit safely in the first three games, and the Giants were up, two games to one. But in the fourth game, Joe came alive, hitting a two-run homer, helping his team to a 6–2 win. In game five, Joe had three hits and the Yanks won 13–1. And in the sixth, after hitting two doubles, the Giants pitchers walked Joe for the rest of the game. They were afraid to pitch to him because they knew what he could do in big games. Even with Joe silenced, the Yankees won the game 4–3 and took the series. It was their third in a row.

After the game, Joe told his teammates it had been his last. He'd won ten pennants and nine World Series, all with the same team. Who could ask for a better record than that?

Chapter | Ten

Two Great Loves

On December 11, 1951, the Yankees held a press conference, and Joe announced that he had played his last game. He was somber and his answers to the many of the reporters' questions were short and curt. "I've played my last game of ball," Joe said. "I just don't have it anymore." An awe-inspiring career had finally come to an end.

The Yankees offered Joe a job doing postgame television interviews with the team the following spring. Joe accepted a one-year contract, figuring he would try out broadcasting. Still, he had a few months before the season started. He ended up spending a lot of time with his friends and family until, in March 1952, he met someone who would change his life forever.

Marilyn Monroe was an up-and-coming starlet in Hollywood. Joe had seen her picture and thought she was beautiful, so a date was set up for them in Los Angeles. They met over dinner with a couple of friends, and Joe was instantly in love. Marilyn was smitten as well, and the famous couple spent almost every evening together after their first date. It was a classic whirlwind romance.

Then in April, Joe had to return to the East Coast for his new job as a Yankee broadcaster. He didn't take very well to the role. Joe had never felt all that at ease when he was being interviewed by other reporters. He had to display the quick thinking of an on-air journalist, and he hated it. When people tried to joke with him, he didn't know how to respond, and that old blushing habit from his childhood would rear its ugly head. He just felt stupid, a feeling he never had been able to stand. Joe decided early on that he wouldn't renew his contract for another season.

Joe DiMaggio was going to take a real break from baseball. Normally stars like Joe were invited back to spring training after their retirement to hang out with the team, inspire them, and maybe coach them a little. But Casey Stengel was still the Yankees manager, and he and Joe were still not talking. As long as Stengel was in charge, Joe wasn't going to show his face in the Yankee dugout.

So instead of being with the team, Joe spent most of his time with Marilyn. In January 1954, after almost two years together, Joe asked Marilyn to marry him. She said yes.

Joe decided that this time he wouldn't risk turning his wedding into a sideshow. Instead he and Marilyn were wed by a judge on January 14, 1954, two days after their engagement. A few members of the press found out about it and managed to be there, but it was nothing like the insanity that surrounded his first wedding. Afterward the newlyweds took off for Japan, where they were greeted by thousands of Japanese fans.

A stretch of the West Side Highway in New York City—the road that Joe often took to get to Yankee Stadium—was renamed Joe DiMaggio Highway.

Unfortunately, things didn't stay rosy for long. Marilyn's star was on the rise, and there were always studio people over at Joe and Marilyn's house. Producers, publicists, dressers, hairstylists, everyone seemed to want time with Joe's new wife, and he often felt crowded out. Joe had wanted a normal marriage and a quiet home life, but it was clear he wasn't going to get one with Marilyn. Their marriage wouldn't last out the year. They divorced in the fall of 1954.

After that, Joe couldn't stay in Los Angeles. He returned to New York and settled into a suite at the Hotel Lexington, but he spent a lot of time traveling, making appearances at various functions and golf tournaments. On July 25, 1955, he was inducted into the National Baseball Hall of Fame.

In 1960 eight of Joe's nine World Series rings were stolen from his suite at the Lexington. Luckily Joe always wore the ring from his rookie season, 1936, so that one was safe and sound. He had held on to the most important souvenir, but it didn't take the sting out of losing the others. Between this and his shunned status with the Yankees, it seemed like the baseball fates were frowning on him.

The following spring, however, baseball opened up to Joe once again. Casey Stengel left the Yankees, and Joe was invited to spring training for the first time since his retirement. The younger players were in awe of him, and Joe felt like he was finally being recognized for all he had done for his team. It was great to be back on the diamond.

 At Old Timers Day games, the retired Yankee greats always gave Joe the first seat in the dugout.

Meanwhile, Joe never got over Marilyn, and in 1962, he finally won her back. They were supposed to be remarried in August of that year, but four days before the wedding, Marilyn was found dead of an apparent drug overdose. Joe was crushed. For the rest of his life, he would send roses to her grave two times each week.

After Marilyn passed away, Joe knew he had to get on with his life. He had been offered various jobs in baseball over the years, but he had turned them all down because of meager pay. But in 1967, he was given an offer he couldn't refuse. The Kansas City Athletics were moving to Oakland, California, right near Joe's hometown of San Francisco. In need of some publicity in their new home, the A's offered Joe a position as vice president. Joe took the job, figuring it would be nice to help out the new home team. Then, during spring training in 1968, he started coaching for them as well. As predicted, his presence on the team did generate some much needed publicity. Joe stayed on with the A's for two seasons and was even there to give a few batting tips to a new rookie named Reggie Jackson. Jackson would go on to become a Hall of Fame hitter.

For the rest of his life, Joe would make most of his money doing commercials for Mr. Coffee coffeemakers and the Bowery Savings Bank. He also gave speeches at various organizations, talking about his glory days in baseball. Joe enjoyed playing in Old Timers Day games at Yankee Stadium, where retired players come to the ballpark and play a three-inning match. He was always happy to throw out first pitches when his presence was requested. Joe knew he represented a golden age in baseball to a lot of people, and he was happy to appear in public for his fans.

❝DiMaggio was the greatest all-around player I ever saw. . . . It might sound corny, but he had a profound and lasting impact on the country.❞

—Boston Red Sox star Ted Williams

When Joe was in his seventies, he started appearing at baseball card shows a few times a year to sign his picture and meet the public. People lined up early and often to meet him.

Then in 1991, the Yankees threw a huge celebration to honor the fiftieth anniversary of Joe's amazing hitting streak. The stadium was sold out, packed with modern-day fans, most of whom had never seen Joe play, but all of whom knew exactly how great a hero he was. Many of his old teammates—including Whitey Ford, Mickey Mantle, and Yogi Berra—showed up too. Joe was showered with gifts and accolades. He stood on the field at Yankee Stadium with a smile on his face and tears in his eyes. He had been booed and cheered here. He'd had some of the greatest moments of his life, and some of the worst, in front of those stands. This was Joe DiMaggio's home, and on that day, he felt as lucky as ever to be a Yankee.

A Hero Lives On

Joe DiMaggio was always wary of lending his name to anything. He constantly received requests from companies wanting to name things after him. From wings of buildings to stretches of road to ballparks to pasta sauces, the requests came in from all over the country, but Joe always refused. He didn't want to cheapen his name. Plus he didn't like the idea of some people he'd never met making money off of him. It just didn't seem fair or right.

In 1992 Joe received a request from Memorial Regional Hospital in Hollywood, Florida. They wanted to name their expanded pediatric unit after Joe, who had made Hollywood his home for the past few years. At first Joe didn't like the idea—his initial reaction was to turn them down, like he always did with such requests. But then he found out the reason behind the proposed change.

The hospital wanted to be able to cover the surgery costs of children whose parents didn't have enough money to pay for vital operations. They wanted to expand their children's cancer and orthopedic surgery facilities as well. They were going to need to raise a lot of money to be able to do these things. The director of the hospital knew that if they had a famous name attached to the ward, like DiMaggio's, it would be a lot easier to raise the money they needed.

Joe wondered why they wanted to use his name above anyone else's, and he was told they had a few reasons. First, he was a local resident and hero. Second, he meant so much to so many people that his name was universally recognized. And third, kids love baseball. What better name for a children's hospital wing than the name of one of the biggest baseball stars of all time?

Joe was flattered and moved by the idea of helping kids who didn't have enough money to pay for treatment. He agreed to let the hospital use his name. After that, Joe wasn't required to do anything for the hospital, but he couldn't just sit back. He knew this was a good cause, and he wanted to show people that he really supported it. Not only did he attend fund-raising events like baseball games and comedy shows but he signed memorabilia to be auctioned off at fund-raisers and occasionally visited the kids in the hospital.

Joe was getting on in years and it meant a lot to him that he could give back to the community in a way that had nothing to do with baseball. Here he was, in the twilight of an amazing, blessed life and he had the chance to help struggling families. Because of his fame, he was able to do something real to help save lives. It meant even more to him than being elected into the Hall of Fame.

Between flying around the country to make appearances, helping out with the hospital, and signing lots of autographs, Joe kept busy in the last years of his life. By September 1998, his health began to fail. He had developed a cough that wouldn't quit, and he wasn't eating or sleeping well. Still, Joe kept up his travels. Over the years, there hadn't been much that would keep him from doing his job, and this illness was no exception.

But when the Yankees told Joe they wanted to throw him a tribute in September of that year, Joe knew there was a good chance it would be his last appearance at his old ballpark. The ceremony was to take place at Yankee Stadium on September 27, 1998, before the last game of the season. Joe was to be presented with eight replica World Series rings to replace those that had been stolen.

Joe spent days working on his speech. After all, this could be his final chance to address the fans. He wanted to get it just right. But the day wouldn't turn out the way he planned. When

Joe stepped up to the microphone to address the capacity crowd of more than 56,000, the microphone didn't work. He was a few lines into his speech when he realized what was happening and stopped. Phil Rizzuto, his old teammate who had come out to honor Joe, walked out onto the field to present the eight World Series rings. Embarrassed, Joe took the rings, waved to the crowd, and left the field.

That October Yankees owner George Steinbrenner wanted Joe to throw out the first pitch of the World Series for the Yankees. It wasn't to be. Instead of heading back up to New York, Joe entered the hospital that October to have a tumor removed from his lung. Over the next few months, he suffered various complications, including infections and pneumonia. He would never return to New York again.

During his last weeks, Joe was visited by various friends and family members, including Steinbrenner and his only living sibling, his brother Dominic. He finally passed away in his hospital bed on March 8, 1999. His final words were, "I'll finally get to see Marilyn again."

Those words may not have been very fitting to those who saw Joe only as a sports star, but those who loved him knew that he had never gotten over Marilyn's death. Just like the fans at the stadium, Joe hadn't had a chance to say good-bye to her either, and he had missed her all those years.

When Joe died, he was wearing his 1936 World Series ring, the ring from the team he had loved more than any other, from the series of which he was most proud. He passed away peacefully, knowing he had made his mark not just on baseball, but on the world.

PERSONAL STATISTICS

Name:

Joseph Paul DiMaggio

Nicknames:

The Yankee Clipper, Joltin' Joe, Joe D., Dead Pan
Joe

Born:

November 25, 1914

Died:

March 8, 1999

Height:

6'2"

Weight:

193 lbs.

Batted:

Right

Threw:

Right

BATTING STATISTICS

Year	Team	Avg	G	AB	Runs	Hits	2B	3B	HR	RBI	SB
1936	NYY	.323	138	637	132	206	44	15	29	125	4
1937	NYY	.346	151	621	151	215	35	15	46	167	3
1938	NYY	.324	145	599	129	194	32	13	32	140	6
1939	NYY	.381	120	462	108	176	32	6	30	126	3
1940	NYY	.352	132	508	93	179	28	9	31	133	1
1941	NYY	.357	139	541	122	193	43	11	30	125	4
1942	NYY	.305	154	610	123	186	29	13	21	114	4
1946	NYY	.290	132	503	81	146	20	8	25	95	1
1947	NYY	.315	141	534	97	168	31	10	20	97	3
1948	NYY	.320	153	594	110	190	26	11	39	155	1
1949	NYY	.346	76	272	58	94	14	6	14	67	0
1950	NYY	.301	139	525	114	158	33	10	32	122	0
1951	NYY	.263	116	415	72	109	22	4	12	71	0
	Total	.325	1,736	6,821	1,390	2,214	389	131	361	1,537	30

Key: **Avg**: batting average; **G**: games; **AB**: at bats; **2B**: doubles; **3B**: triples; **HR**: home runs; **RBI**: runs batted in; **SB**: stolen bases

FIELDING STATISTICS

Year	Team	Pos	G	C	PO	A	E	DP	FLD%
1936	NYY	OF	138	369	339	22	8	2	.978
1937	NYY	OF	150	451	413	21	17	4	.962
1938	NYY	OF	145	401	366	20	15	4	.963
1939	NYY	OF	117	346	328	13	5	2	.986
1940	NYY	OF	130	372	359	5	8	2	.978
1941	NYY	OF	139	410	385	16	9	5	.978
1942	NYY	OF	154	427	409	10	8	3	.981
1946	NYY	OF	131	335	314	15	6	3	.982
1947	NYY	OF	139	319	316	2	1	0	.997
1948	NYY	OF	152	462	441	8	13	1	.972
1949	NYY	OF	76	199	195	1	3	0	.985
1950	NYY	OF	137	381	363	9	9	1	.976
		1B	1	13	13	0	0	0	1.000
1951	NYY	OF	113	302	288	11	3	3	.990
	Total		1,722	4,787	4,529	153	105	30	.978

Key: Pos: position; G: games; C: chances (balls hit to a position); PO: putouts; A: assists; E: errors; DP: double plays; FLD%: fielding percentage

SOURCES

4 Richard Ben Cramer, *Joe DiMaggio: The Hero's Life* (New York: Simon and Schuster, 2000), 172.

9 Morris Engelberg and Marv Schneider, *DiMaggio: Setting the Record Straight* (St. Paul: MBI Publishing Company, 2003), 211.

11 Cramer, *Joe DiMaggio,* 13.

18 Engleberg, *DiMaggio,* 216.

20 Cramer, *Joe DiMaggio,* 42.

20 Joseph Durso, *DiMaggio: The Last American Knight* (Boston: Little, Brown, 1995), 31.

25 Bill Madden, *Pride of October: What It Was to Be Young and a Yankee* (New York: Warner Books, 2003), 91.

26 Ray Robinson and Christopher Jennison, *Pennants & Pinstripes* (New York: Viking Studio, 2002), 57.

29 Cramer, *Joe DiMaggio,* 74

30 Ibid.

30 Ibid., 85

31 Durso, *DiMaggio,* 68.

33 Engleberg, *DiMaggio,* 23.

37 Durso, *DiMaggio,* 90.

38 "Quotations From Joe DiMaggio," *baseball-almanac.com,* n.d, http://www.baseball-almanac.com/quotes/quodimg.shtml (January 18, 2005).

42 Cramer, *Joe DiMaggio,* 117.

50 "Quotations About Joe DiMaggio," *baseball-almanac.com,* n.d, http://www.baseball-almanac.com/quotes/quodimg.shtml (January 18, 2005).

52 Durso, *DiMaggio,* 133.

53 Harvey Frommer, *The New York Yankee Encyclopedia* (New York: Macmillan, 1997), 20.

53 Durso, *DiMaggio,* 135.

55 "Quotations About Joe DiMaggio," *baseball-almanac.com,* n.d, http://www.baseball-almanac.com/quotes/quodimg.shtml (January 18, 2005).

63 Durso, *DiMaggio,* 157.

68 "Quotations About Joe DiMaggio," *baseball-almanac.com,* n.d, http://www.baseball-almanac.com/quotes/

quodimg.shtml (January 18, 2005).

71 Cramer, *Joe DiMaggio,* 248.

73 Robinson, *Pennants & Pinstripes,* 95.

77 Durso, *DiMaggio,* 179.

77 Cramer, *Joe DiMaggio,* 273.

80 Engleberg, *DiMaggio,* 61.

81 Ibid., 65.

82 "Quotations From Joe DiMaggio," *baseball-almanac.com,* n.d, http://www.baseball-almanac.com/quotes/quodimg.shtml (January 18, 2005).

83 Cramer, *Joe DiMaggio,* 296.

86 Engleberg, *DiMaggio,* 67–68.

87 Durso, *DiMaggio,* 204.

92 "Quotations About Joe DiMaggio," *baseball-almanac.com,* n.d, http://www.baseball-almanac.com/quotes/quodimg.shtml (January 18, 2005).

96 Engleberg, *DiMaggio,* 384.

BIBLIOGRAPHY

Cramer, Richard Ben. *Joe DiMaggio: The Hero's Life.* New York: Simon and Schuster, 2000.

Durso, Joseph. *DiMaggio: The Last American Knight.* Boston: Little, Brown, 1995.

Engelberg, Morris, and Marv Schneider. *DiMaggio: Setting the Record Straight.* St. Paul, MN: MBI Publishing Company, 2003.

Ford, Whitey, with Phil Pepe. *Few and Chosen: Defining Yankee Greatness Across the Eras.* Chicago: Triumph Books, 2001.

Frommer, Harvey. *The New York Yankee Encyclopedia.* New York: Macmillan, 1997.

Madden, Bill. *Pride of October: What It Was to Be Young and a Yankee.* New York: Warner Books, 2003.

Robinson, Ray, and Christopher Jennison. *Pennants & Pinstripes: The New York Yankees 1903–2002.* New York: Viking Studio, 2002.

Stout, Glenn. *DiMaggio: An Illustrated Life.* New York: Walker, 1995.

Viola, Kevin. *Lou Gehrig.* Minneapolis: Lerner Publications Company, 2005.

Zoss, Joel and John S. Bowman. *The History of Major League Baseball.* New York: Crescent Books, 1992.

WEBSITES

New York Yankees: The Official Site

http://newyork.yankees.mlb.com

The official Yankees site has a ton of history, including articles about Joe.

Baseball Almanac: Joe DiMaggio

www.baseball-almanac.com

Search for Joe DiMaggio and find some great quotes and statistics. This site also has the lyrics for the song "Joltin' Joe."

The Sporting News

www.sportingnews.com/archives/dimaggio/index.html

The website of Joe's favorite magazine includes a whole section devoted to Joe.

Baseball Library: Joe DiMaggio

www.baseballlibrary.com

Search for Joe DiMaggio and you'll get a page that features a great timeline of Joe's career.

INDEX

A
All-Star Game, 32–33
American League, 32–34, 85
Angels, Los Angeles, 29
Athletics, Kansas City, 91

B
Bagby, Jim, 53
Barrow, Ed, 25–26, 29–30
Bauer, Hank, 81–82
Bees, Boston, 31
Berra, Yogi, 83, 92
Bevens, Bill, 69
Bowery Savings Bank, 91
Browns, St. Louis, 2–3

C
Cardnals, St. Louis, 57
Cavney, Ike, 18, 20–22
Cobb, Ty, 29, 46
Combs, Earle, 2
Crosetti, Frank, 44
Cubs, Chicago, 43–44

D
Daniel, Dan, 30
Dead Pan Joe, 24, 30
Derringer, Paul, 47
Devine, Joe, 25
Dickey, Bill, 35, 47, 51
DiMaggio, Dominic, 8,
    13–14, 48, 52–53, 60,
    76
DiMaggio, Dorothy Arnold,
    40, 45, 48–50, 56–57,
    59–65
DiMaggio, Frances, 8
DiMaggio, Giuseppe, 6–13,
    17–18, 41, 74–75
    Rosalie D., 7
DiMaggio, Joseph Paul
    All-Star Game, 32–33
    childhood, 6–14
    early baseball, 8–9,
    14–18
    Hall of Fame, 90
    hitting streaks, 1–5,
    23–24, 50–54, 82
    Galileo High School,
    10–1

Hancock Elementary, 8
Joe DiMaggio Day, 76
Joe DiMaggio's Grotto,
    41
Jolly Knights, 14–5
nicknames, 17, 24, 30,
    52, 63, 98
retirement, 81–82,
    86–87
Seals, 17–29
statistics, 98–100
U.S. Army, 57–62
World Series, 34–37,
    40, 43–44, 46–47,
    54–55, 57, 69–70, 78,
    85–86
Yankees career, 1–5,
    25–57, 61–97
DiMaggio, Joseph Paul, Jr.,
    56, 60–1, 64
DiMaggio, Mamie, 8
DiMaggio, Marie, 8
DiMaggio, Michael, 8, 10,
    13, 38
DiMaggio, Nellie, 8
DiMaggio, Rosalie Mercurio,
    6–, 13, 76, 84, 96
DiMaggio, Tom, 8, 10–1, 13,
    21, 41
DiMaggio, Vince, 8, 11–4,
    17–8, 22, 60
Dodgers, Brooklyn, 54–55,
    69–70, 78

E
Eckhardt, Oscar, 29

F
Flood, Brigadier General
    William, 58
Ford, Whitey, 62, 83, 92

G
Galan, Augie, 19–21
Galileo High School, 10–11
Gehrig, Lou, 30, 35, 39,
    41–43, 49, 51, 68
Gehringer, Charlie, 40
Giants, New York, 35, 37,
    40, 60, 85–86

Gomez, Lefty, 65
Gordon, Joe, 54–55
Graham, Charlie, 21, 26
Great Depression, 22

H
Hancock Elementary, 8
Harris, Bucky, 4, 67, 73
Heinz, 54
Henrich, Tom, 5, 55–56
Hoag, Myril. 34
Hopp, Johnny, 85
Hubbell, Carl, 35

I
Indians, Cleveland , 2–3, 49,
    53, 85

J
Jackson, Reggie, 91
Jackson, Travis, 29
Joe DiMaggio Day, 76
Joe DiMaggio's Grotto, 41
Jolly Knights, 14–15

K
Keeler, Wee Willie, 3, 5
Keller, Charlie, 46–47, 55

L
Lumber League, 11

M
MacPhail, Larry, 65–66
Manhattan Merry Go Round,
    40
Mantle, Mickey, 84, 92
McCarthy, Joe, 31, 34, 42,
    45–46, 50–51, 53,
    65–66
McCormick, Mike, 58
Memorial Regional
    Hospital, 93–94
Monroe, Marilyn, 87–91, 96
Mr. Coffee, 91

N
National Baseball Hall of
    Fame, 90
National League, 32–34

O

O'Doul, Francis "Lefty,"
28–29

P

Pacific Coast League, 17
Page, Joe, 70–71
Passarella, Art, 68
Pearson, Monte, 46
Peckinpaugh, Roger, 2
Phillies, Philadelphia, 60, 83
Pirates, Pittsburgh, 60
Priddy, Gerry, 58

R

Rizzuto, Phil, 96
Reds, Cincinnati, 46–47, 58
Red Sox, Boston, 5, 39, 43,
48, 52, 60, 66, 75–80,
85
Rosalie D, 7
Rossi Olive Oil Co., 15
Ruffing, Red, 30, 46, 54–56,
58, 68
Ruppert, Colonel, 41–42, 44
Ruth, Babe, 29–30, 39, 56

S

San Francisco Chronicle, 24
Seals, San Francisco, 17–29
Senators, Washington, 3–5,
52, 58, 66
Shea, Spec, 70
Sisler, George, 3, 52
Smith, Al, 53
Sporting News, The, 24–25
Stars, Hollywood, 22
Steinbrenner, George, 96
Stengel, Casey, 73–74,
80–82, 85, 88, 90
Sunset Produce, 15–16

T

Terry, Bill, 37
Tigers, Detroit, 35, 49, 51,
68
Turbeville, George, 59

U

U.S. Army, 57–62

V

Venezia, Frank, 14

W

White Sox, Chicago, 1–2
Williams, Ted, 92
Window Breakers, 44
World Series, 34–37, 40,
43–44, 46–47, 54–55,
57, 69–70, 78, 85–86
World War II, 51–52, 56–57

Y

Yankee Clipper, 63
Yankees, New York, 1–5,
25–57, 61–97